WARRIORS OF THE RAINBOW

Strange and Prophetic Dreams of the Indians

By William Willoya and Vinson Brown

Major Artists

Tzo Yazzie (Navajo), Jim Redcorn (Osage)
Al Momaday (Kiowa), Clayton Sampson (Paiute)

DEDICATED TO:

Freedom and Justice for all the Indian peoples.

Third Printing

Published by Naturegraph Company, Healdsburg, Calif.

TABLE OF CONTENTS

FOREWORD

In the words that follow we have written simply and wholly what we believe, believing that only God is the Knower. That men should love one another and understand one another is the great message of the visions of the Indian peoples told about in this book, nothing of selfishness nor vanity, nothing of narrowness nor pride. We write what we feel deep in our hearts, and the bulk of the book is the expression of this feeling. On the other hand, we wish to write about only what is reasonable and intelligent, so, in the appendix at the back of this book, we give what we consider reasonable and intelligent answers to why the study of prophetic dreams has value, how they fit patterns, and how it may be possible to understand them.

People more interested in the spirit will turn to the beginning of the book first, but those more practical and critical might do well to read the appendix first. Each part has its place in this book, each answers a need. The subject is a deep one and only a beginning is given here. We hope that the reader of this book will continue to investigate the ideas offered in these pages with an open mind. For the light of truth shines best through open minds.

These visions come not only from the American Indians, but from the Indians of India and from the East Indian Islands. While these Indians of Asia are not of the same cultural background as the Indians of America, both have one thing in common. They were both conquered and treated badly by the white people. It is remarkable that among all these Indian peoples their great prophetic dreams do not speak of how revenge will some day come for their humiliation, but how there will one day be brotherhood and love between all races. It is the bigness and grandeur of these visions that makes any forward-looking person want to help them come true, for they promise the spiritual regeneration and uplifting of all mankind.

"A new thing came and they could not see,
A new wind blew and they would not feel it."
From the poem, In His Own Country, by Lord Dunsany.

I. THE RETURN OF THE SPIRIT

Drawn by Major Osborne Cross - 1849

"Once we were all free on the prairies together,
Blue and rose and yellow prairies like this one.
We ran and chased and hunted.
You were good to us.
You gave us food and clothes and houses.
Now we are all old.
We are tied,
But our minds are not tied.
We can remember the old days.
We can say to each other,
Those times were good."

"Of course you don't understand my singing," Spear Woman said (as she sang to the buffalo behind the fence). "Of course you don't know what it's about when I sing about the old days. You're just calves. You don't remember. You were born inside the fence, like my own grandchildren."

Quoted from The Ten Grandmothers, by Alice Marriott, University of Oklahoma Press, 1945, with kind permission of the Publishers.

(NOTE: The story told below we believe actually happened, though not in these exact details. We have deliberately named no tribe in this story because we want it to mean the same to all tribes, to all the Indians, for a wise old woman anywhere and a boy who had curiosity and spirit anywhere could find together this same miracle. This story makes live for us the heart of the message given us in all the great Indian prophetic visions told about in this book.)

The old woman sat under the shade of the cottonwood tree by the creek and nodded her head, dozing a little. She was very old, so old that the wrinkles made little fine ridges all

over her face and her eyes seemed hidden among the ridges
like springs lost in a desert.   But, when a sand lizard ran
among some rattleweed, brushing their stems, and causing
the pods to rattle a little in the windless air, she opened her
eyes and they peered out from among the folds of skin, bright
and glowing with life like two points of black desert opal
sparkling in the sun.   Eyes of the Fire she had been called
long ago when she was seventeen and danced on the prairie
while half a dozen fine young hunters pressed forward to woo
her.   But that was long, long ago, in the days when the white
men were still few in number and the Indians yet had some
of their ancient freedom.

Now an Indian boy of about twelve summers came wandering down to the creek, a little self-conscious in store clothes,
but his eyes gazing about him full of wonder.   He was Jim,
her great grandson, recently come from the city where his
father worked as a mechanic in a big garage, new to the mountain country, new and strange, and a little bit afraid of the
other Indian boys, his relatives, who lived there.   It was getting near to midday and the other people had gone indoors to
snooze through the heat, but Jim walked slowly and   shyly
down to the creek beside his great grandmother.

Little flashing lights of laughter raced through the eyes of
the old, wise one.   She saw the wonder in him as he gazed at
the mountains with their snow on top, and said tenderly:

"What do you want, Jim?"

Dust jumped in little spurts as the boy kicked the ground,
and his lips trembled.   Then they firmed as he looked straight
into the lively old eyes.

"I want to ask a question, Oldest Mother."

"Ask then," she said quietly and suddenly her body seemed
to grow less old, and it appeared almost as if she were sitting
straight in a saddle on a spirited horse as she had done many
a time in the long ago.

"Last night you told us stories," said the boy, and you could
see in the eager reach of his eyes, the clenching of his fists,

how he had sat tensely in the firelight of the previous evening drinking into his very pores the tales of old. "Last night you told of how the white man came and took our land, of how the Indians were struck by diseases until their bones became so weak that thousands died, of how great-grandfather was killed by a white man because he tried to stop a robbery. All these things that you told us about, Oldest Mother, make me want to ask you something."

"Ask then!" she commanded, and her voice was like the wind in the mountains. The boy drew back, as if he would run, but he clenched his hands again and spoke.

"Why did our Grandfather in the sky allow the white men to take our lands, Oldest Mother?"

Eyes of the Fire became as still as a desert fox crouched at the hole of a kangeroo rat. Only the eyes remained alive and moving, watching the boy as if she had seen him for the very first time. She saw the fine eyes and the proud way he held his head, the nose of him a little big, but strong and bold, and she saw in him something of his great-grandfather as he had been in his youth when the hunter's glow was about him and he came in proudly through the sagebrush with an antelope over his shoulder.

"You are the first to ask that question," she whispered. "Your father and your grandfather never asked such things. Why do you ask?"

"Because I want to know?" he cried impatiently. "Why have there been such bad things happen to our people? Why? Why?"

Again the old one became very still. Again she looked at him long and silently. Could it be? she asked herself, that the spirit is returning? Could it be? Could it be? Something grew inside of her, something so strong and powerful, that it roared inside of her like the wild grass fire. It thundered as mustangs do when they stampede down to a water-hole. It had been a small thing before, that hope, only a tiny flicker of flame, nourished somewhere deep within her by the stories of the ancient ones, the wise story tellers, keepers of the traditions of her people. She remembered the fires by the tents of long ago, the coyotes howling and laughing in the circling dark, and the mountains, great lumps to northward, from whence the winds shrieked down with their touch of ice. She remembered shivering deliciously on the edge of the light and the warmth, just a small girl person, unimportant in the tribe, but for awhile caught up with past glories and the great dreams. Yes, the hope was growing, it was springing within her, like hunters coming home with buffalo rumps and tongues on their saddles and the wild, wild shouting. But she dared not let the hope show in her eyes, she dared not! There would be a long time yet before she could be sure. This was only a soft little boy from the city; time would tell if his will was strong.

She realized suddenly that Jim was looking at her eagerly.

"Listen, boy who speaks his mind, this is a big question you have asked me. This is a question to be asked by a warrior, not a boy. When a boy your age asked such a question in the old days, the wise chiefs looked at him and said: 'Ho, what a big question from a little one! Let us test him before we answer, let us send him into the wild places to find his spirit. Only big people can have an answer to such a question. Let us see if he is big.'"

"What do you want me to do, Oldest Mother?"

The question startled the old one. She had not expected it, but now her eyes crinkled and she began to laugh. Somehow it was not an old woman's laugh. Somehow it breathed the wild laughter of the mountain winds, somewhere within it was the cry of the eagle and the scream of the mountain lion, somewhere also was deep pride that a boy child of her blood should ask such things.

But suddenly Eyes of the Fire grew worried.

"What I want you to do, and what your mother and father will let you do may be two different things."

The boy laughed defiantly.

"My mother and father want to lie in the shade and sleep. Or they want to watch the TV or listen to the radio. They have come to rest this summer, they say. But I want to run in the hills and watch the animals. Tell me what you wish me to do, Oldest Mother, and then answer my question. It will be a secret between us."

The old, wise one shook her head.

"Look at me, Jim," she commanded. "Do you really want to know the answer to your question? Do you really want to know why the Spirit of All let the white men take our lands?"

The boy nodded his head eagerly and looked straight into her eyes. Then he took a knife from his pocket and suddenly cut his finger. Triumphantly he cried:

"See, Eyes of the Fire," and it was the first time he had used her old name. "I have cut myself even as the old ones did when they sought visions. In my blood I have written my answer. Tell me what I must do!"

Tears rushed to her eyes. Blindly she reached out to touch him.

"Thank the One in the Sun I have lived to see this day! Go tell your mother and father that I want to see them."

She sat up very straight, like a chief at the time of decision, like a warrior drawing his arrow.

The boy ran and his feet kicked up happy clouds of dust. He was no longer the city boy, afraid of the strange things around him, shy and unsure of himself. He was like his great grandfather in the long, long ago, joyously running down his first jackrabbit.

When the young mother and father came slowly and protestingly down to the cottonwood tree, led by their eager son, they saw immediately that the old woman was not as they had known her. Her eyes sparkled and flashed. Even her body, old and bent as it was, seemed strangely young and vigorous.

"What do you want, Grandmother?" the man asked. He was stocky and strong, but he bowed his head a little in spite of himself, as one does to a great and wise chief, and his hands were nervous, for he saw the eagle look in her eyes.

"Sit down and listen to me, " the old one commanded.

They seated themselves in the grass, as cicadas shrilled in the cottonwood trees and the creek murmured over its sand.

She pointed to the boy.

"This one has asked me a question that is important. But it is so important that I can only give the answer to a purified one, a spirit seeker. "

"Oh Grandmother!" protested the young woman, "those things are of the long ago. We live in a new time now. "

The old woman seemed to grow bigger before their eyes. She took a stick and made a mark in the sand. It was the ancient mark of their people, and a sign made with the hands, when two strange tribesmen met.

"For eighty years, " she said slowly, "I have been waiting for this day. For eighty years I have seen the spirit of my people slowly being killed by the white men. For eighty years I have seen my people trying to follow the white man's ways. Some of these ways have been good. Some have been very bad. But worst of all has been the going away of the spirit of our people, for a people are nothing when the spirit is gone."

"But we have learned the white man's religion, " protested the man. "There is much good in his religion. "

"There is much good in his religion, it is true. But most white men use their religion as a child uses a toy. When the white man thinks it is useful to him, he remembers it, but when it interferes with his pleasure, he forgets it. In the old days we Indians helped each other in trouble; even the weakest were helped; we really lived our religion. Then the white men came with ambitions to change the ways of the Indians. When they brought love, as some few did, this was good, but when they brought the breaking up of our people into many little religions, and laughed at our religion, this was bad. Jesus never taught these little things that divide the white men and divide the Indians who listen to them. His love was too big for such small things.   Let the white men learn again the truths of their own religion and no longer will they build walls between themselves and between other peoples of the world."

The man looked at the ground.

"What do you want us to do?" he asked reluctantly.

"Let the spirit of this boy grow. Let it grow as big as the sky! I will send him to the mountain tops and to the strange places. He will learn the secrets of our people that you and your father have long forgotten. He will bring back the spirit that is almost lost.   Long ago the ancient ones told me that these things would be. The white man would kill the spirit of the Indian peoples, and take it to a far place, but after awhile it would come back again, it would be born again. In time a new spirit would come to the world, they said, and we should look for it. Like the rain drops gathering in the clouds of the springtime so would the spirit come to a thirsty land and a dying people. It would bring back life and hope and make them great again.   I have seen the beginning of this spirit in this boy. Let it grow! Let it grow!"

The old woman was very tired by her long talk, but her eyes still glowed like shining coals. Suddenly the young man remembered her as he had when a child and a great sense of loss came to him. In the deepest part of his heart, he whispered to himself: "I should have listened to her when I was young. Now it will be my son who will have the honor." He saw that his wife was about to protest again, for there was fear in her eyes and her lips moved.   He touched her gently with his hand.

"The old one speaks the truth," he said.   "When we shall look deeply we shall understand.   It is a great privilege the boy has been offered."

"I will learn," said the boy, and he stood as straight as a spear.

Even the young woman began to look at him with pride, and for a time they were all silent.

That night the old one told stories by the fire again and the children sat very still as they listened, their eyes big in the gleam of the flames. And it seemed that there was in the air a new thing, a new feeling, as if the spirit of the Indians, withdrawn far into the mountains, hidden in the mountains, came down into the valley again.

The next day Jim was awakened at dawn by a touch on his shoulder and looked up into the wise old eyes.   He leaped to his feet, ready for the whispered command. He jumped into the cold dawn water of the creek and washed himself.   He heard the meadowlark calling his morning song, and lifted his facing shining to the first red rim of the sun, asking good of all being. He ran on bare feet to the hills and his feet hurt a little, but he did not cringe. At the top of the hill he lifted his arms and prayed toward the sun, to our Grandfather in the sky, an old, old prayer that Eyes of the Fire had taught him.   For ten more days he ran in the hills, till his thighs jumped beneath him as they do in antelopes springing over the prairie.

In the middle of the tenth night the old hand touched him, and he rose trembling to go out into the darkness. He knew that this was the test for courage and he clenched his teeth, thinking of eyes in the bushes and furred bodies, of the poisoned teeth people, the rattlesnakes, and the shadows.

"Pray to the Spirit of all Life for protection, " said the old one.   "Remember the animals and the Indians are brothers. If your heart is good, nothing will harm you.   Do not worry about sticks and things in the darkness, but walk like a man and bring to me from the top of the highest hill a rock that strikes fire. "

As Jim walked through the dark night toward the hills, he trembled and looked about wildly. He banged his head on a branch, tripped on a rock, and fell, sprawling, into a prickly bush. A scream fought up in his throat, but he forced it back as a road runner seizes and forces back a striking rattlesnake.   All around him he heard strange noises and rustlings. In the distance a coyote howled like a lost devil child and he was sure he heard the foot-falls of a panther creeping softly beside him in the stillness. Then, even as he wished to cry for help and run back to the house, he heard in his mind the voice of his Great-grandmother saying: "If your heart is good, nothing will harm you. The Indians and the animals are brothers."

The spirit leaped like a stallion within him and he said a little prayer as he gazed up at the stars. He also whispered an ancient song of past warriors: "The night is my friend, for it hides me, and I am a wolf in the nighttime."

Now proudly he stepped through the starlight. He came to a clump of juniper trees and he walked among them without a branch touching him, for his body seemed as fluid as creek water. He began to run with feet that felt as if they had eyes in their toes, and his body sensed every rock and shrub and tree he passed. He flashed up the last bit of steep climb to the hilltop without panting. He seized a rock and knew by the feel of it that it was a fire stone. His fingers scrabbled over ground for another rock of the same kind, and he struck the two together until they made a shower of sparks. Far below, he saw an answering light from the valley and he sucked in his breath, knowing with joy that sang that the old one watched.

He laughed aloud, for he knew he had passed the first difficult test and he thrust his arms out into the coolness of the wind. All the darkness was full of little voices talking, whisperings and rustlings, squeakings from under the bushes, and, in the far distance, an owl hooting weirdly. Once he had shivered at these sounds, but now they seemed to be saying over and over, "Jim has won! Jim has won!"

Day and night the training went on. He learned to lie perfectly motionless watching a squirrel until he knew all its habits. Day and night muscles and mind and soul were toughened, and his spirit grew. After three weeks the old, wise one felt the muscles in his legs and arms. They were as hard as the black obsidian rock.

"Make your own bow and arrow," she said. "Forget the guns of the white men. They are only cold steel, but the bow of the Indian has a soul; it comes alive in his hands. And the making of a bow, the very task done in love and worship, puts the strength of the Spirit within you. When you have made a bow your father cannot break, then bring me a deer from the mountains, remembering an Indian kills only for things that he needs.

Jim had never made a bow before. The first one broke in his hands, when he pulled on it. The second one, the old one told the father to test and, in the hands of the strong man, it snapped in two. In secret Jim wept because that bow had taken a long time to make and he was tired of bow making. The old one told him to go to a certain cave in the hills where he found a branch of seasoned hard wood and brought it back to the house. Stubbornly he gritted his teeth and set to work on the wood, but feeling the job was endless.   Suddenly, on the second day, the old Indian spirit of craftsmanship settled upon him. Cutting, filing, smoothing, he began to see the grain of the wood turn beautiful under his hands as it took on the shape of the ancient bow of his great-grandfather, a bow that hung under the smoked black rafters of the house by the creek.

This third bow did not break when the man tried it. It was strong and true and its bowstring of sinew hummed threateningly when Jim pulled it.   Following the old one's instructions, he made arrows out of willows and mountain mahogany and feathered them with turkey feathers.

He went into the hills to practice because he wished no one to see him. At first the arrows went every way but the way to the target and many arrows were broken. Grimly Jim made more arrows, and slowly he grew better. His arm was raw where the bowstring struck it, until he learned to put on a guard of leather. At last he learned to hold two arrows in his mouth while shooting the first and soon could wing all three arrows singing into the target within a dozen seconds' span.

Two nights later he was alone in a canyon of the mountain, looking into the dancing flames and seeing the ancient hunters gather around him in the flickering shadows to give advice. He bent his head and prayed the age-long prayer that the deer people would forgive him for his kill, that he would partake of their strength and courage by eating their flesh, that his heart would be good.

Trees and shadows and grass merged with his spirit in the new dawn; the creek, laughing down over its rocks, sang in his blood; the movement of dark forms at the edge of a meadow in some cottonwoods keyed his nerves to tight alertness. Rocks and sharp leaves scarred his knees as he began his stalking.   But he poured all his soul into his hunting until he became a part of the earth, until his brown body merged with leaf and rock and trunk as if no human being were there.

How his hand shook when he rose at last from behind a boulder and drew the arrow to its notched head, gazing down the waving line of it at the tan shoulder of a young buck! Suddenly the white tail flashed and the buck jumped away, hooves pounding. A new power surged into Jim and his heart let out a great shout as he heard the arrow sing its deadly song.   It struck the fleeing buck and Jim plunged after it, shouting.

Suddenly he saw the deer lying near him under a bush, blood gushing from its mouth, and its great dark eyes flooding with pain and terror.   And, in those eyes, when he got close, he saw all the pain of countless animals wounded in the past by men, lying, writhing in traps, or with shattered limbs, and he knew suddenly what he had never understood before, why the wise Indians of old killed only in need for food or clothing or in self defense.   Even as he struck the blow that brought a merciful end to pain, his heart leaped with a great and silent prayer. He prayed that this would be the last time he needed to kill and that, instead, he would help protect and bring back to the earth the animals that the white men had almost destroyed. He made a sign his people used only when making a sacred vow, promising the Great Spirit to make it so.

"It is well," said the old, wise one, when Jim laid the meat and skin before her late that evening, "he is beginning to be a man." She tossed some sacred seed on the fire until the flame blazed cherry red, but he was so silent that she looked long into his eyes until she understood and touched him gently.

"This one has seen pain in others, " she said solemnly. "Look you tonight, oh people, " and her voice rose thrillingly, "like a wise chief, this boy has been close to the heart of the Silent One and his spirit will be great in the years to come. "

In the warm silence the others understood. Into the still-ness a drum began its thumping, and the people started to sing with the wonderful, lifting spirit of the days when the prairies had no fences, but were clean and beautiful for a thousand miles!

Still the training went on, the climbing of cliffs, the search for food and medicinal herbs, the watching, the running, until one day Jim stood before the old one with firey eyes.

"Tell me now, Oldest Mother, why did the Old Man, the Lord of the Lightning, let the white men take our lands?"

She laughed the long, hearty laugh, the deep, wonderful laugh that is heard only when the people know that just friends are about. She reached down with a stick and drew in the dust until she showed a mountain top and the figure of a man standing on the mountain with his arms reached to the sky.

"You have climbed and you have hunted, you have searched and you have found. You have made your muscles like the mountain lion's and your eyes like the eagle's. You have done all these things and there is only one last thing you must do to become a true man, and that is climb to the top of the great mountain over there and eat no food and pray for a vision to come to you from the Spirit of all Things. But, before you do that, I am going to tell you why the Oldest One let the white men take the land of the Indians. Sit and be still! For all I shall tell you will help you to find your vision.

Jim sat and was as still as the wolf cub when its mother sounds the deep growl that means danger is near. Eyes of the Fire made circles in the dust with her stick and then drew a big circle that surrounded all the little circles.

"These little circles are all the little nations and all the little religions of the world, but the big circle is the one big nation and the one big religion that encloses them all, and means them all and knows them all just as a mother quail draws all the chicks of her brood under her spread wings and loves them all as a mother should.

"Long ago, all our people were united in love and knowledge. The wise old chiefs and the wise old women taught the chil-dren how to grow up and be good and to love one another. All the land belonged to all the people and all the children felt that everyman or woman was a father or a mother. So there was no hurt child wandering alone and unloved, and there was no old person who did not have people who looked after him or her. When the young, strong hunters went out to kill buffalo or antelope or deer or elk, they would bring back to the old people, and to the widow and the weak, the best of the meat. So there was kindness and goodness and unity among the people, and there were almost never any thieves or murderers or others like them who do so much harm to people these days."

"But what about wars with other Indians?" asked Jim.

"It is true that sometimes there were wars, but these were very few before the white men came. You must know that the white men came from across the great ocean and then gradually moved west. As they moved, they drove the Indians before them, so that tribes were shoved against each other and began to fight to protect their villages. The more the white men shoved, the more fighting there was until finally there was fighting everywhere. Then the white men brought their whisky that drove the Indians crazy so that they did foolish things that never were done in the ancient days."

"But now tell me, Oldest Mother, why did the Spirit of the Earth let the white men take our people's lands?"

Eyes of the Fire laughed again, a laugh like thunder in a distant canyon, and hid her mouth with her hand, rocking a little from side to side.

"All these things I have told you will help you to understand," she replied. "The old wise ones told me long ago why the white men were sent. The Heart of all Being sent them because the white men come from a land where only white men lived and it was necessary for them to come to this place where they would learn about other races and learn to live with them, and that one day, when the Indians got the old spirit back again, they would teach the white men how to really love one another and how to love all mankind. Now, because the Indians were humbled and made poor by the white man's conquest, they have been cleansed of all selfish pride. They are ready for a great awakening and they will awaken others.

"In their dreams the old ones saw that the Indians would go through a very bad time, that they would lose their spirit, that they would be split up into many parts by the different kinds of religion of the white men. Like the white men, they would try to find what these strange people call success. But one day the Indians would begin to wake up, the old ones told me. They would see that those white people who chased after personal pleasure left behind the truly important things in life. The Indians would see that their people in the old days were in tune with something far more wonderful, the Spirit of Life.

"And you must realize that this is not all the old ones saw in their dreams. They saw that just when the Indians seemed to be all becoming like the more foolish white men, just when everybody thought they had forgotten about the ancient days, at that time a great light would come from the east. It would come into the hearts of some of the Indians, and they would become like the prairie fire, spreading not only love between all races, but also between the different religions.

"This light you must find, oh son of my son's son, my be- loved, and I believe that when you seek for your vision on the mountain top you will be told how to find it. For it will be something so big and wonderful that in it all peoples of the world can find shelter. And, in that day all the little circles will come under the one big circle of understanding and unity."

As she stopped talking, the old woman and the boy looked to the east and they saw a great rainbow flaming in the sky where a thunderstorm had passed.

"The rainbow is a sign from Him who is in all things," said the old, wise one. "It is a sign of the union of all peoples like one big family. Go to the mountaintop, child of my flesh, and learn to be a Warrior of the Rainbow, for it is only by spreading love and joy to others that hate in this world can be changed to understanding and kindness, and war and destruction shall end!"

"And it shall come to pass afterward, that I will pour out
my spirit on all flesh; your sons and your daughters shall
prophecy, your old men shall dream dreams, and your young
men shall see visions." Joel, 2:28.

SEEKING FOR THE RETURN OF THE SPIRIT

Listen, oh my ears, listen, as the fawn listens for its
mother in the forest, but listen, my ears, for the Words
of the Spirit.

Watch, oh my eyes, watch, as the otter watches over his
children, but watch, my eyes, for the Way of the Spirit.

Feel, oh my fingers, feel, as the lair cub feels the warm
tongue of the bear, but feel, my fingers, the Touch of
the Spirit.

Day by day, I shall gather strength from Thee, thinking,
thinking, but stilling my thoughts, as the calm of
summer stills the waters of a pond.

When my heart is quiet, when my thoughts are still, when I
have forgotten my pride, when I am filled with love for
all Your creatures, lead me oh Grandfather.

In Thy love I shall grow, oh Ancient One, until hatred disap-
pears, until all envy and jealous and petty thoughts are
blown away as the wind blows the fog from the valley.

I was weak, but now You make me strong; I was proud, but
now I shall be humble; I was filled with bad thoughts, but
now they shall be gone forever, even as the wise youth
leaves the ways of childhood and becomes a man.

I am longing, oh Grandfather, for Thy spirit; into the silent
places I go seeking, even as the Eagle Chief climbs
toward the sun.

Down into sleep I will go with my mind at peace; into the
darkness I shall go and shall fear no evil.

On the feet of my breath I shall cross the skies and the vast-
ness of space shall be as the hollow of my hand through
which I pierce as the lightning touches earth and sky.

Then will come Your spirit, oh Center of all Being; as the
light of the outer world fades, the light of the inner world
shall glow, and I shall be swept as on waves of glory into
Thy nearness and Thy knowledge.

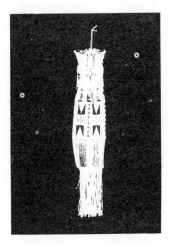

STRANGE DREAM OF THE OGLALA SIOUX PIPE BAG

(This account told by Vinson Brown.)

Photo of Oglala Sioux pipe bag given author's father when he was in South Dakota. Photo by Charles Bello.

For me this story began when I was a small boy of five and my father showed me a wonderful bag, a bag made of soft doe-skin, about four feet long and covered with beautiful beaded designs, glowing in green, blue, white, red and gold. When I touched that bag a flame of wonder seemed to dart up my arm and into my heart.

My father told me that this was a pipe bag of the Oglala Sioux and had been used by them to carry a special pipe, used in ceremonies. In the early 1890's my father was a doctor on the Sioux Reservation at Pine Ridge, South Dakota. You must understand that in those days the Sioux were a conquered people, suffering under the white man's laws, and looking at the barren prairies with unseeing eyes, remembering sadly the days when the buffalo were everywhere and the hunters could roam wild and free.

One day, when the snow of winter was lying deep over the dead grass, a chief of the Oglala Sioux sent a message to my father, asking him to come and try to save the life of his son, who was dying of pneumonia. When my father came and saw the little boy lying wrapped in a buffalo robe

with his face flushed with fever, he vowed he would do everything possible to save his life. He stayed awake for two days
and nights, working on the boy, rubbing his chest with cod
liver oil, and giving him what medicine he thought would help.
In the middle of the second night the boy appeared to be dying,
and my father, in desperation, put his lips to his mouth and
blew into it to force air into his lungs. Somehow this helped
and later, no longer able to stay awake, my father fell into
an exhausted sleep.

When he awakened, the boy had started to recover from his
sickness. A few days later, when the boy was getting well, the
chief and his wife were very grateful and the chief asked my
father what he should pay him for his work.   My father remembered the stories about all that the Indians had suffered.
He said to the chief:

"The white man has always taken things from the Indians.
It is time for a white man to give.   I give you your son's life
and there is no charge."

The chief was too proud to take something for nothing. He
asked his wife to bring out the beautiful pipe bag.   He insisted on giving this to my father to show his gratitude.   He
told my father that the bag had once been thrown on a great
pile of Indian things gathered by white soldiers, and the whole
pile set afire to help crush the Indians' spirit.   But a wind
had come and blown the bag off the pile to a place where the
Indians found it and saved it.

My father was surprised and asked the chief why he was
giving him such a valuable bag, and the chief told him that in
a dream he had been told to give it to the first white man who
did something kind for his family, because some day his giving this bag would bring good to the Indians.   My father told
me that one day the beautiful bag would be mine, and   that,
if my heart was good, he felt the bag would be of help to me.

Soon after my father had shown me the pipe bag and told
me this story I began to have my strange dream.   Over and
over the dream came to me, always exactly the same in every
detail, from the age of five to the age of nine.

In my dream I seemed to be floating in the sky looking down at a land of many round hills. On the top of each hill was a group of Indians. Some of them were lying on the dry grass, with their fingers digging into the ground despairingly. Others lifted their arms hopelessly to the sky. Women were huddled together, weeping. All were wearing old, caste-off white men's clothing, just rags. Their faces were filled with a deep sadness, and their skin seemed drawn over the bones, so that I felt both bodies and souls were hungry.

There seemed to be growing a strange light up in the sky. Looking up, I saw the sunlight flashing on the wings of a beautiful white bird, a dove. The dove circled down from the sky, its body and wings pure as new-fallen snow. Fluttering and circling it came slowly, but there was a feeling about it of immense power, as if all that was in the sky centered upon it.

As the dove came near the top of one of the hills, a strange and remarkable thing happened. The Indians there suddenly sprang to their feet, gazing up at the dove. The white men's rags fell from their bodies and disappeared. Instead they now lifted their heads proudly under handsome headdresses and their bodies were covered with clean buckskin that glittered with beads and with buckles of shell. Their faces glowed with happiness and joy. Their bodies arched like bows drawn back to send forth humming arrows. Then, to my amazement, they began to march up into the sky after the dove, marching with the springing steps of conquerors, like lords of the world.

As the dove dipped low again and again, other dark-skinned peoples rose joyously from hill after hill and marched up into the sky, following the beautiful white bird. I saw many costumes in my dream, but I did not know what they meant or what tribes they represented, only that feathers were waving, beads of many colors glittered, and brown arms gleamed with bronze and gold. Drums began to mutter, lifting and rolling into thunder, and pipes shrilled with triumph. Voices chanted ancient songs and shouted age-long cries of the peoples.

Slowly a bow formed in the sky, a rainbow of people marching to glory, a rainbow of unity and a vision so marvelous in its sense of beauty and joy that I can never forget it nor hope to see anything its equal. Slowly, at the end of each dream, this vision of glory would fade away, but the promise of it always remained, the promise of a wonderful change coming.

For four years I had this dream every few weeks until, when I was nine years of age, it stopped as suddenly as it had begun. I spent the summer of my ninth year on a huge ranch in southern Nevada called the Hot Creek Ranch. It was about seventy miles long by sixty miles wide. I learned to ride half-wild horses, bare-back and with saddle, while the wind whistled in my ears. I remember the smell of the sagebrush, spicy and wild, the shouting and laughter of clear mountain streams leaping down waterfalls, and the happy way we whooped when we tried to run down antelopes or mustangs.

I danced with excitement when another boy on the ranch invited me to ride with him to visit a small Shoshone Indian Reservation a few miles away. It was a great adventure on the way to see those few Shoshone families, but, when I arrived, the day became dark and terrible. Once the Shoshones were a fine people, brave and good, filled with the wonderful spirit of the wild places. I found them living in broken-down shacks, wearing white men's caste-off, ragged clothing. On their backs rested a burden of woe, and their eyes looked only at the ground.

It is strange that I did not realize then that these people I saw were just like the Indians had appeared at the first in my dream, filled with a great sadness, their spirit and hope killed by the white men. I rode away from there sick in my heart, and, because I did not understand, my dream stopped.

Many years later I came to know other Indians and I found very fine ones. I understood also how my own people had crushed and hurt the Indians. In the jungles of Panama I met a Burica Indian who still had all the spirit of the old days. He led me into the forest and coated my clothing and skin with the strong smell of a plant that killed the man odor. He told me to be still. I was quiet as a fawn when danger rustles in the bushes. Then he called the animals and birds out of the trees. His voice warbled and chuckled and whispered like all the

voices of the woods. Birds like flames of fire flew down to
perch on his shoulders. Great black howling monkeys, their
throats throbbing out deep, gurgling cries, swung down   the
vines to shout and grunt at him.   Later, long-nosed coati-
mundis, cousins of the raccoons, came to nuzzle his knees,
and he played with them as a child plays with a puppy or a
kitten. I watched this wonderful sight with awe, hardly dar-
ing to breath because I was afraid I would disturb it.   This
man had a great spiritual power, so close was he to the
Breath that breathes through the wilderness.

Later still I was traveling all over the western part of the
United States lecturing at schools. I met a number of Indians
on this trip and told several the story of my dream.   I
asked them what it meant, but, for a long time, none could
tell me.   Then, one day, when I was driving from Albuquer-
que, New Mexico, to Snowflake, Arizona, I came far out into
the desert and saw a tall young man striding down the road
ahead of me with the long, springing steps of a runner. He
was not asking for a ride, but accepted one when I offered it,
saying he was walking to take a job at a ranch ten miles ahead
and had covered already twenty miles of the journey.   His
face was strong and good, his eyes flashing with spirit. He
said he was mainly Otomi, of a tribe that lives in the mountains of central Mexico, but part Olmec. When he heard my
story of the strange dream, his face suddenly shone with understanding!
                                              10 and 42
"I know what your dream means!" he cried.   "Long ago
there lived a great prophet-king of the Toltec Indians of southern Mexico called Quetzalcoatl, which means the 'Feathered
Serpent'. Quetzalcoatl brought a message of love and kindness, teaching the people how to make new things and to raise
better crops, and making the Toltecs into the greatest nation
of Mexico. My grandmother told me that there was an ancient
story that, as Quetzalcoatl left the Toltecs to journey to a far
place, he prophecied what was going to happen to the Indians.

"He foretold that in time white men would come out of the
eastern sea in great canoes with white wings like a big bird.
These were the sails on the ships of those days. He promised

that the white men themselves would be like a bird that had
two different kinds of feet.   One foot would be the foot of a
dove and the other the foot of an eagle.   The foot of the dove
meant the religion of Christianity, which was brought by the
white men, and which is a religion of love and kindness, although too few of the white men lived by this religion.   The
foot of the eagle meant the way most of the white men treated the Indians, by clawing them, killing them, enslaving them
and exploiting them.

"But Quetzalcoatl promised the Indians that a few hundred
years after the first coming of the white men other white men
would come to the Indians with both feet the feet of the dove,
and that either Quetzalcoatl himself or the spirit that was in
him would return at this time.   This means, from what you
saw in your dream, that new white men would come in the
form of a white dove.   They would lead the Indians up from
the earth of despair and defeat into the sky of hope, freedom
and triumph.

"The fact that the Indians you saw in the sky were wearing
the clothes of the ancient days meant that these white men
would not make fun of or laugh at the old Indian culture and religion.   Instead they would teach the Indians to be proud of
their ancestors and get back the great spirit and knowledge
the ancient people had.   As true brothers, both the Indians
and these white men would start to build a better world in
which justice, peace and love between men would rule. "

Long have the words of the Otomi echoed in my ears, and
long has my heart yearned to understand even more fully the
meaning of my dream.   Somehow, William Willoya, the Eskimo, has come to help me with this search.   The results of
our search appear in this book and we hope will lead others
to seek for and understand the great spirit of change that
is even now growing in the world.

"There ariseth a little cloud out of the sea, like a man's
hand. " I Kings, 18:44.

III. INDIAN PROPHETIC VISIONS

We believe there is a great strength in the earth and in nature that the old Indians knew about, but which is almost all lost to present generations.[7] This power of the spirit gained from the wilderness most people who live in cities know nothing about. The farmer who loves the soil in which he works has some of this feeling, for the spirit of growing things becomes deeply meaningful to him. He senses their needs and works to meet them, which produces a successful farm.

We who have lived in the wilderness for long periods, as have both the writers of this book, experience after awhile a strange feeling of kinship with the life there that causes one's whole being to become sensitively attuned to both wild life and plants. After awhile, if the heart expresses love towards the wild creatures, more and more of them will begin to befriend you and the harmony of all life becomes visible.[32] The Indians, if we can believe the stories of the ancient wise ones, went a step beyond this to the point where the human spirit in some way, possibly never measurable by scientists, used the animal spirit as a tool in reaching the Source of the World and in purifying the soul.[7] The great, pure-hearted chiefs of the olden times achieved their spiritual power by the most difficult self-discipline, fasting and prayer, including the utter emptying of the heart of all earthly desires and the tuning of the inner ear to the whispers of the wilderness. This was not idol-worship, as many who did not understand them often believed, but something far deeper and more wonderful, the understanding of the Spirit of Being that manifests itself in all living things. From this deep understanding we believe they sometimes had actual flashes of insight into the future of their people and the world. These prophetic visions of times of great trouble to be followed by a time of world harmony and peace form the remarkable patterns of thought and beauty that you will find in most of the stories that follow.

A. PROPHECY OF MONTEZUMA, AZTEC KING

The Aztecs were a civilized but warlike Indian people of central Mexico who inherited their culture from the wonderful Toltec Indians.   The Toltecs had been given a religion of kindness and goodness by their prophet-king, Quetzalcoatl. It is too bad the Aztecs did not fully learn this religion.   Instead, they began to change it and introduced human sacrifice.   They cut out the hearts of thousands of their enemies to sacrifice to their war god, Huitzlipotchli.

Montezuma II was the king or emperor of the Aztecs when the white men, the Spaniards, came. Like most of the Aztecs of that time, he took part in the wars, bringing thousands of of that time, he took part in the wars, bringing thousands of captured warriors to be sacrificed at the great temple of the war god. For a time he was a cruel king, glorying in his power over other Indians. But when the Spaniards, led by Cortez, came and captured Montezuma, they treated both him and his people badly. He began to turn again to the religion of Quetzalcoatl. More and more he became troubled and sick in his heart as he saw the white men killing thousands of the Indians in the name of Christ, cutting them down with their guns and steel swords.

When Montezuma tried to stop the fighting, he was badly wounded by one of his people. As he lay dying, the Spirit sent to Montezuma a wonderful vision of the future, which the king told to his favorite daughter, Tula. Later Tula passed on the story of this vision to Iztlilzochitl, a noble Tezcucan Indian, who wrote this prophecy down in a book.

"To the world I have said farewell, " said Montezuma. "I see its vanities go from me one by one. Last in the train and most loved, most glittering is power, -- and in its hands is my heart. A shadow creeps upon me, darkening all without, but brightening all within; and in the brightness, lo, I see my People and their future!

"The long, long cycles -- two, -- four, -- eight -- pass away, and I see the tribes newly risen, like the trodden grass, and in their midst a Priesthood and a Cross. An age of battles more, and, lo! there remains the Cross, but not the priests; in their stead is Freedom and God. "

"I know the children of the Aztec, crushed now, will live, and more, -- after ages of wrong suffered by them, they will rise up, and take their place -- a place of splendor -- amongst the deathless nations of the earth. What I was given to see was revelation. Cherish these words, O Tula; repeat them often, make them a cry of the people; a sacred tradition; let them go down with the generations, one of which will, at last, rightly understand the meaning of the words FREEDOM AND GOD, now dark to my understanding; and then, not till then, will be the new birth and new career. "

Now is come a generation of Indians that can understand Montezuma's prophetic words FREEDOM AND GOD. A great new spirit is now spreading over the world that rises above the petty misunderstandings, prejudices and hates of the past. To find the truth of this Spirit, each person must cast out of his mind and soul the walls of religious misunderstanding that keep men apart, and search freely, independently and joyously for the truth. In earlier ages it was necessary to have special religious leaders who led the human flocks and did most of their religious thinking for them, but in this age of greater maturity we must all grow up and think and seek for ourselves until we find the glorious light of brotherhood that awaits us.

26

*B. VISION OF PLENTY COUPS, CHIEF OF THE CROW

Indian dancer being decorated. Photo of drawing made for Bureau of Ethnology Smithsonian Institution, Washington, D. C.

Plenty Coups was a very wise and great leader of the Crow or Absorokee Indians of Montana and Wyoming. He was not only successful in leading his people through the troubles of war but also through the even more difficult troubles of peace after the white men had conquered the west.

When Plenty Coups told the story of his life to the plains-man and mountain man, Frank B. Linderman, he told also the story of his great vision. Plenty Coups was about nine or ten years old when the dream came to him. He had gone into the Crazy Mountains in Montana to seek a vision, and fasted for several days. He grew very weak, but still had no dream. Finally, in desperation, remembering how the great Crow warriors of the past showed their courage, he cut off a joint of his index finger and forced it to bleed. He fell asleep and then seemed to wake up to find himself surrounded by war ea-gles. Later a spirit person came to him and led him through a long tunnel underground in the direction of the Arrow Creek Mountains, and he found himself surrounded by many buffalo jostling against him in the tunnel. At first he was very much afraid they would crush him, but the spirit person told

* Shortened version of story told, starting on page 60, in AMERICAN, the Life Story of a Great Indian, by Frank B. Linderman. The John Day Co., 1930. Used with kind permission of the publishers.

him to walk straight ahead and have no fear.

When the spirit being led him out of the hole into the sun-slight, the spirit person shook a large red rattle and sang a queer song four times. "Look!" he pointed, and Plenty Coups saw thousands of buffalo coming out of a hole in the ground, blackening the plains. Then suddenly they seemed to disappear. Now, out of the same hole, came great herds of spotted and horned animals, that he understood later were white men's cattle. These bellowed and snorted, but differently from the buffalo, so that he was frightened by their appearance and sounds. Soon they too disappeared, but accomplished the change by going back into the great hole in the ground.

"Do you understand this which I have shown you, Plenty Coups?" asked the Spirit Person, but the boy answered "No!"

The Spirit Being led Plenty Coups back through the hole in the ground to a place that is now on the Crow Reservation in Montana and showed Plenty Coups an old man sitting feeble and alone in the shade.

"This old man is yourself, Plenty Coups," said the Spirit Being, who soon disappeared along with the old man.

Now Plenty Coups saw a dark forest with a black storm coming. The four winds struck the forest with a great roaring and the boy felt pity for the living things there. The winds tore down all the trees except one, which stood tall and straight. "What does this mean?" whispered the boy.

"Listen, Plenty Coups," said a spirit voice. "In that tree is the lodge of the Chickadee. He is least in strength but strongest of mind among his kind. He is willing to work for wisdom. The Chickadee-person is a good listener. Nothing escapes his ears, which he has sharpened by constant use. Whenever others are talking together of their successes or failures, there you will find the Chickadee-person listening to their words. But in all his listening he tends to his own business. He never intrudes, never speaks in strange company, and yet never misses a chance to learn from others. He gains success and

avoids failure by learning how others succeeded or failed, and without great trouble to himself.   There is scarcely a lodge he does not visit, hardly a person he does not know, and yet everybody likes him, because he minds his own business, or pretends to.

"The lodges of countless Bird-people were in that forest when the Four Winds charged it.   Only one is left unharmed, the lodge of the Chickadee-person.   Develop your body, but do not neglect your mind, Plenty Coups.   It is the mind that leads a man to power, not strength of body."

After this Plenty Coups wakened and was helped by his friends back to the Crow camp. All the wise men of the tribe gathered together in a great lodge and called Plenty Coups to come there and tell them about his vision.   As he told his story, he could feel the excitement in the air for this was a very unusual dream.   They sat silent for awhile, smoking; then, Yellow Bear, the wisest, slowly rose and spoke:

"He has been told that in his lifetime the buffalo will go away forever, and that in their place on the plains will come the bulls and cows and the calves of the white men.   I have myself seen these Spotted-buffalo drawing loads of the white man's goods --

"The dream of Plenty Coups means that the white men will take and hold this country and their Spotted-buffalo will cover the plains.   He was told to think for himself, to listen, to learn to avoid disaster by the experiences of others.   He was advised to develop his body but not to forget his mind.   The meaning of his dream is plain to me. I see its warning.   The tribes who have fought the white men have all been beaten, wiped out.   By listening as the Chickadee listens we may escape this and keep our lands.

"The Four Winds represent the white man and those who will help him in his wars. The forest of trees are the tribes of these wide plains. And the one tree that the Four Winds left standing after the fearful battle represents our own people, the Absarokees, the one tribe of the plains that has never made war against the white man.

"The Chickadee's lodge in that standing tree is the lodges of this tribe pitched in the safety of peaceful relations with the white men, whom we could not stop even though we would. The Chickadee is small; so are we against our many enemies, white and red. But he was wise in his selection of a place to pitch his lodge. After the battle of the Four Winds he still held his home, his country, because he had gained wisdom by listening to the mistakes of others and knew there was safety for himself and his family. The Chickadee is the medicine of Plenty Coups from this day. He will not be obliged to carry a heavy medicine bundle, but his medicine will be powerful both in peace time and in war.

"He will live to be old and he will be a chief. He will someday live differently from the way we do now and will sit in the shade of great trees on Arrow Creek, where the Manperson took him in his dream. The old man he saw there was himself, as he was told. He will live to be old and be known for his brave deeds. --- I have finished."

From the time of this dream the Crow Indians began to cooperate with the white men, understanding that they could not fight against them. The result is that today the Crow Reservation in southern Montana on the Bighorn and Little Bighorn Rivers is about the finest Indian land in the west.

Plenty Coups great wisdom in watching carefully and learning from the mistakes of others allowed him to guide his people through troublous times. He showed great sharpness of mind when he described the white men as follows:*

"They spoke very loudly when they said their laws were made for everybody, but we soon learned that, although they expected us to keep them, they thought nothing of breaking them themselves. They told us not to drink whiskey, yet they made it themselves and traded it to us for furs and robes until both were nearly gone. Their Wise Ones said we might

* *Taken from page 227 of the book, AMERICAN, the Life Story of a Great Indian, by Frank B. Linderman. John Day Company, 1930; with kind permission of the publishers.*

have their religion, but, when we tried to understand it, we
found that there were too many kinds of religion among the
white men for us to understand, and that scarcely any two white
men agreed which was the right one to learn. This bothered
us a good deal until we saw that many white men did not take
their religion any more seriously than they did their laws,
and that he kept both of them just behind him, like Helpers, to
use when they might do him good in his dealings with strangers. These were not our ways. We kept the laws we made
and lived our religion. We have never been able to understand the white man, who fools nobody but himself. "

Comment on the vision of Plenty Coups.

The message that came to Plenty Coups was similar to the
message given Montezuma, but Plenty Coups had more of it
explained to him. Montezuma was promised that the Indians
would begin to awaken when they understood the meaning of
"Freedom and God." Plenty Coups was actually taught how
to use some of this freedom of the spirit. He was told, of
course, how to learn from the mistakes of others, but his
lesson really went much deeper than this, for he was warned
that the people who did not learn to think independently and
develop their minds would go down before the storms of life.

This is what has happened to so many of the Indian people.
They have been so thrown out of their ancient way of life by
the white men's influence that it has been a great shock to
them. They have thought to themselves that there is nothing
for them to do but copy the white men's way of living, because the past is gone forever. Of course the old ways will
never come back exactly as they were, but the spiritual power and the goodness and kindness and courage that were in the
Indians of old can come back.

Plenty Coups was told that one of the ways to keep the Indian spirit alive was to learn to think independently and to
search for the truth with an open mind. This is the strengthening of the mind that he was told was more important than
the strengthening of the body. No mind is a powerful mind,
a strong mind, unless it is also a seeking mind. The seeking
mind finds truths and applies them to life and the problems
of the world .

"SPIRIT COUNCIL," Jim Redcorn (Osage). Shows the eagle and b
gone into the wilderness to fa

followers of the new light from the Great Spirit (symbolized
nisunderstanding and pleasure-seeking into the sky of glorious
and love.

"THE WARRIORS OF THE RAINBOW," Tzo Yazzie (Navajo). The
by the white dove) are rising from the earth of heedlessness,
unity, purity

...ffalo gens (spirits) counseling the Tzi-shu chief. The Indian has
...t and pray for spiritual help.

C. PROPHECY OF KING DJOJOBOJO

Buddha's Lotus Throne, supported by Nagas, Serpent Men. From painting on wall of Kanheri Cave in India.

From Buddhist Art in India, by Albert Grunwedel, 1901.

Buddha taught love and understanding about 550 B. C.

The people of the island of Java and other islands around it are called East Indians. They appear to be a brown-skinned people, but are actually a mixture of several races and some pure types of these races appear on the islands. Originally there were the Negritos, or black-skinned people, but pure examples of these people are found now only in the wildest parts of the high mountains of Sumatra and Borneo. The Malay peoples, who are part of the Yellow Race, like the Chinese and Japanese, are now the most numerous people on the islands, but there is also mixed in with them some blood of the White Race, though the people of white blood who first came to Java from India over two thousand years ago appeared more brown than they did white.

Four great religions have come to the East Indian Islands, each started by a famous Prophet or Messiah who taught people to live in love and harmony. First there came the Hindus from India, whose Prophet was Krishna, and who taught people to:

"Be humble, be harmless, have no pretension;
Be upright, forbearing; serve your teacher in true obedience,
Keeping the mind and the body in cleanliness,

"Tranquil, steadfast, master of ego, standing apart
From the things of the senses, free from self;[62]
Aware of the weakness in mortal nature --. " *

Second, there came the Buddhists, also from India, whose
Prophet, Guatama Buddha, was believed by the Buddhists to
be the return of Krishna. Buddha taught such things as:

"Not to commit any sin, to do good, and to purify one's
mind, that is the teaching of all the Awakened. "
"Not to blame, not to strike, to live restrained under the
law, to be moderate in eating, to sleep and sit alone, and to
dwell in the highest thoughts -- this is the teaching of the
Awakened One. " ** [63]

Third, there came the Moslems from Arabia, with Islam,
the religion of the Prophet Muhammad, who taught men to:

"Seek help in patience and in prayer, and truly it is hard
save for the humble-minded. " The Koran, Surah II: 45.
"And feed with food the needy wretch, the orphan, and the
prisoner, for the love of Him (God), saying: we feed you for
the sake of God only. We wish for no reward nor thanks from
you. " The Koran, Surah LXXVI: 8-9.
"O my people!   Give full measure and full weight in justice, and wrong not people in respect of their goods. And do
not evil in the earth, causing corruption. " Koran, Surah XI:
85. *** [68]

Fourth, there came the Christian Dutch from Holland, who

* From page 101 of THE SONG OF GOD, BHAGAVAD-GI-
TA, translated by Swami Prabhavananda and Christopher Isherwood. Mentor Books and Harper & Bros., 1951. Quota-
tion used with kind permission of the publishers.

** From page 61 of THE TEACHINGS OF THE COMPAS-
SIONATE BUDDHA, edited by E. A. Burtt. Mentor Books,
New Am. Library of World Literature, Inc., 1955. Quota-
tions used with kind permission of the publishers.

*** Selected from THE MEANING OF THE GLORIOUS
KORAN, translated by Mohammed M. Pickthall. Mentor Books,
New Am. Library of World Lit., 1953. Quoted with kind per-
mission of the publishers.

conquered the East Indian Islands, but brought the good words
of the Prophet Jesus, who said:

"But I say unto you, love your enemies, bless them that
curse you, do good to them that hate you, and pray for them
which despitefully use you, and persecute you." Matthew 5:44.
"Judge not, that ye be not judged. For with what judgment
ye judge, ye shall be judged." Matthew 7:1-2.

In spite of the fact that all four of these great Prophets
taught their people to deal kindly with other people, and not
to speak evil of others, their followers in the East Indian Islands, as elsewhere, often fought with each other and hated
each other, refusing to try to understand each other's religions. Is this not astonishing and also very childish?

When we understand about this hate and prejudice and misunderstanding between these four great religions, then we can
understand how remarkable was the strange prophecy of the
great Indian King, Djojobojo, who lived on the island of Java
during the twelfth century A. D.[58] King Djojobojo was a good
and just ruler, who did everything possible to make his people
happy. He himself apparently belonged to the Buddhist religion, while most of his people were Hindus. But he treated
people of all religions with equal kindness and goodness.

One night King Djojobojo fell asleep after long fasting and
had a strange vision in which he saw the future of the Indian
people of his islands rolled out before him like a carpet. He
is believed to have caused this great vision to be written down
and it reads approximately as follows:[50]

After a few centuries, he said, the islands would be conquered by white-skinned, fair-haired, blue-eyed men from the
northwest who would rule the Indians of the islands with an
iron hand for about three hundred and fifty years. (The col-
onial rule of the white men, or Dutch people, actually lasted
from 1610 to 1942 or 332 years.) He foretold that the white
men would be driven off the islands by slant-eyed, yellow-
skinned dwarfs from the northeast (these were the Japanese,
who conquered the islands in 1942 during the Second World
War), but he said the dwarfs would stay on the islands for

only a very short time, for little more than one planting of
the corn! (The Japanese were quite amazed during the time
they ruled the islands to see the East Indians so carefully
planting corn! And, sure enough, in four years the Japanese
in turn were driven off the islands. This happened in 1946, at
the end of World War II.)

After the dwarfs had left, said the king, the East Indians
would be ruled by their own people, but this would be a very
bad time for brother would fight against brother, religion
against religion, race against race, and social groups against
other social groups. Blood would flow. (This is what has been
happening on the East Indian Islands since their independence
from the white men and there has been much trouble and blood-
letting, hate and misunderstanding between the different social movements and religions of the islands.)

However, prophecied King Djojobojo, this time also would
not last very long. Soon word would come from a great Spiritual King in the west (that is toward the Holy Land) that would
unite all the religions, all the races and social groups, bringing a thousand years of peace.

Comment on the Djojobojo Prophecy.

Notice that it is highly unlikely for this prophecy to be fulfilled by any of the four older religions because the prejudices and misunderstandings between them are too deep. The
Christian missionary, for example, tells the Buddhists, Hindus and Moslems, that their religions are wrong and only his
is right. This immediately builds a wall of anger.

The only way this unity can come is through understanding
and love on such a big scale that the petty misunderstandings
and hates of the past fall away before it like ice before the
sun.   The remarkable thing is that today this fourth step of
the prophecy is actually beginning to happen in the East Indian
Islands.   There are teachers there now, the new teachers,
bringing a great Message of love and harmony between   all
religions and all peoples, attacking no religion of the past,
but saying all are from God.

D. PROPHECIES OF KRISHNA AND BUDDHA,
GREAT INDIAN PROPHETS

1864 lithograph of Krishna, from Hindu Pantheon by Moon.

We give these prophecies together, because they are tied
closely to each other and because the prophecy of Krishna is
very short. Krishna, the Prophet of the Hindu Religion, is
an almost mythological figure, so far back in the misty past
of the sub-continent of India that it is hard to know just when

He existed, though it was probably before 1000 B.C. Wonderful stories are told about Him, including how he saved a countryside from a terrible storm by holding up a mountain between the earth and the rain clouds (shown in picture).

Probably the beautiful essence of Hinduism, as distinct from the crude additions later put into it by men, is expressed in a part of the majestic Hindu poem, the Mahabarata, where a magic crane asks a wise Indian prince:

"What is the road to heaven?"
"Truthfulness, " the prince answers.
"How does a man find happiness?"
"Through right conduct. "
"What must he subdue, in order to escape grief?"
"His mind. "
"When is a man loved?"
"When he is without vanity. "
"How does one reach true religion?"
"Not by argument. Not by scriptures and doctrines; they cannot help. The path to religion is trodden by the saints (by those only who live lives of goodness and purity). " *[68]

Another part of the Mahabarata is called The Bhagavad-Gita, the Song of God. This is so utterly beautiful and so filled with wisdom and love that it is astonishing that people of other religions cannot see that this too comes from God. In this Song, Krishna is reported to speak to the Prince Arjuna of the Bharatas, and tells him: [68]

"Whenever there is decay of righteousness, O Bharata, and there is exaltation of unrighteousness, then I Myself come

---

* Quoted from THE SONG OF GOD, BHAGAVAD-GITA, as translated by Swami Prabhavananda and Christopher Isherwood. Mentor Books, 1951, with permission of publishers.

forth; for the protection of the good, for the destruction of evil-doers, for the sake of firmly establishing righteousness, I am born from age to age. "*

This prophecy of Krishna did not mean that He Himself, the exact same individual, would return from age to age, but that God would again speak through the voices of great Prophets in future ages. If we understand this, we can see that Buddha (born about 563 B. C.) was a return of Krishna, as was also Jesus and Muhammad. The proof of all these great Prophets lay in their Messages of goodness, kindness and honesty, and that from Their teachings rose great world civilizations in which human beings learned to cooperate together as never before. If we can understand how this can be so, then we can realize that the Return of Jesus, spoken about in the Bible, can be thought of as not the return of the same individual, but of the same spirit of God, speaking through a Man, a Prophet. The Bible illustrates the misunderstanding about this when Jesus (in Mark 9:11-13) implies that John the Baptist is the return of Elias, the ancient Jewish prophet, for whom the Jews were watching as a forerunner of the Messiah. Since John the Baptist himself denied that he was Elias (John 1:21), this is strong evidence that, while John the Baptist was not the same individual as Elias, Jesus believed that he received the same kind of message from God that Elias had received. He was, therefore, spiritually the same as Elias, but not physically or even mentally the same.

This idea helps us understand the prophecies of Buddha. Buddha was born the Prince Siddartha, son of an Indian King of the Sakya Clan or Tribe, sometime in the first half of the Fifth Century, B. C. He was raised in luxury at the foot of the wonderful Himilaya Mountains, the highest mountains on earth, and was trained to become a powerful king. But something more powerful drove him to seek for the truth. He left all his luxuries and earthly power behind him and wandered in the wilderness, praying and meditating. One day, when he was

* *Quoted from the BHAGAVAD-GITA, as translated by Annie Besant.*

sitting and thinking for hours under a magnificent Bo tree, God came to Him in a vision and told Him he was to be the Buddha, the Light of Asia, and one of the great world Teachers or Prophets.

1864 lithograph of the Great Prophet, Guatama Buddha.

Buddha went forth among men and began to teach them a Message of love and understanding. He taught them the famous Eight Fold Way that leads to true happiness. This is:

1. <u>Right understanding.</u> You should understand yourself and others clearly and intelligently, so you can make wise choices.

2. <u>Right purpose</u> (aspiration). You should aim not at personal pleasure, but at the good and well-being of all mankind.

3. <u>Right speech.</u> You should speak only goodness and kindness to others.

4. <u>Right conduct.</u> The wise person is always honest, trustworthy, loving and kind.

5. <u>Right vocation.</u> The wise person never does foolish work that hurts other people in any way.

6. <u>Right effort.</u> The wise person works with love; he does the best job he can and always finishes what he starts.

7. <u>Right alertness.</u> He is alert to ward off evil and do good.

8. <u>Right meditation.</u> His thoughts are under control and always are pure and good.

This Teaching is similar to that of many of the great, pure and wise Indian chiefs of America. Any person who studies the life and sayings of Buddha with an open mind will find only good in them and great wisdom. He will see that this Man also came from God, just as did Jesus and Moses. God has sent Teachers to many parts of the world to help man, just as He has sent His rain and His sunlight and wind.

Buddha knew that after a long time His religion would begin to lose strength and would no longer be answering the new problems of the world as it should. He knew that other Buddhas or Prophets of God would appear to help men with new lessons. He knew that eventually a great Prophet would come who would unite all the religions and peoples of the world in love and brotherhood. In the same way Jesus foretold of the Day when there shall be "one fold and one shepherd" (<u>John</u> 10:16). Thus Buddha prophesied:[62]

"I am not the first Buddha who has come upon the earth, nor shall I be the last. In due time another Buddha will arise in the world, a Holy One, a supremely enlightened One, endowed with wisdom, auspicious, embracing the Universe, an incomparable Leader of men, a Ruler of angels and mortals. He will reveal to you the same eternal truths, which I have taught you. He will establish His law, glorious in its origin, glorious at the climax and glorious at the goal in the spirit and in the letter. He will proclaim a righteous life, wholly perfect and pure, such as I now proclaim. His disciples will number many thousands while mine number hundreds. "

Amanda, His disciple, then asked him: "How shall we know Him?" And the Blessed One answered:

"He will be known as Maitreya. "

The word "Maitreya" has different meanings. Commonly it means "the Buddha who returns" and, in this sense, means the coming of a new Prophet of God. But, in another sense, it means the "World Uniter. " Thus, while Jesus and Muhammad can be thought of as the return of the spirit that was in Buddha, and so were new Buddhas (Prophets), they were not World Uniters because the world of their times was too much divided and separated by great geographical distances as well as by the lack of education and understanding of the people who lived then to become united. By the time Christianity and the Moslem religion had come in contact with Buddhism, they had become so badly disorganized by the petty divisions of the different denominations that they had lost the strength needed to convert the Buddhists. Thus the world-uniting Buddha (or Prophet) is still awaited by the Buddhists, but the following prophecy shows how they expect Him to come.

In 1929, Professor Nicholas Roerich of Austria came back from explorations in the Himilaya Mountains north of India and wrote a book called ALTAI-HIMILAYA, A Travel Diary.[54] In this book he wrote of a remarkable Buddhist prophecy he had found in high Himilayas, and which the people there believed was soon to come true. This is how he words it:

"It is told in the prophecies how the new era shall manifest itself: 'First will begin an unprecedented war of all nations. Afterward brother shall rise against brother. Oceans of blood shall flow. And the people shall cease to understand one another. They shall forget the meaning of the word Teacher. But just then shall the Teachers appear and in all the corners of the world shall be heard the true teaching. To

this word of truth shall the people be drawn, but those who
are filled with darkness and ignorance shall set obstacles.
As a diamond glows the light on the tower of the Lord of Shambala (the Prophet of the New Age). One stone on His finger
is worth more than all the world's treasures. Even those
who by accident help the Teachings of Shambala will receive
in return a hundredfold. Already many warriors of the teaching of truth are reborn. Only a few years shall elapse before
everyone shall hear the mighty steps of the Lord of the New
Era. And one can already perceive unusual manifestations
and encounter unusual people. Already they open the gates
of knowledge and ripened fruits are falling from the trees.

" 'The Banner of Shambala shall encircle the central lands
of the Blessed One (Guatama Buddha). Those who accept Him
shall rejoice, and those who deny Him shall tremble. -- The
denier shall be given over to justice and shall be forgotten.
And the warriors shall march under the banner of Maitreya
(the World Uniter).

" 'From the west, from the mountains, shall come my people. Who shall receive and safeguard them? Thou? ' "

Comment on the Buddhist prophecies.

First, note that the prophecies say the new teachers come
from the west (as did the Djojobojo prophecy, given on page
34). Since several of the American Indian prophecies say the
teachers or light will come from the east, this shows a center for the new religion east of the United States and west of
Central Asia. A map illustrates this on page 90.

We are now living in the time after the Great World Wars
when the new teachers are coming to all the world to spread
the new message of unity and understanding between all men.
Unlike the religious teachers of recent centuries, who have
unfortunately brought division and misunderstanding among
men by the insistence of each group of them that they alone
have the truth, the new teachers bring harmony and love. It
is their desire to understand every man and they shall con-
demn no man. The warriors of the Prince of Peace are coming, and before them the walls of misunderstanding shall fall.
Their footsteps are thundering on the spirit-rim of the World.

E. VISION OF DEGANAWIDA
PROPHET OF THE IROQUOIS

Old print of Iroquois chief, from early nineteenth century. Reproduced in LEAGUE OF THE IROQUOIS.

About a hundred years before the white men came to what is now the state of New York, the Iroquois-speaking nations of that area were at war among themselves and also with their

Algonquin-speaking neighbors. Alarmed at this warfare and disunity, and apparently given visions by God, a wise Huron Indian, called Deganawida, began to preach a religion of love and harmony among the tribes. He found no one to listen to him among his own people, the Hurons, but, when he visited other Iroquois tribes, such as the Mohawk, the Onondaga, the Seneca, the Cayuga and the Oneida peoples, his ideas were welcomed. These tribes formed the Iroquois confederacy.

Among these Indians was a young man named Hiawatha, who had led a bad life, but he became Deganawida's chief disciple and helped him greatly in spreading the new religion. Deganawida and Hiawatha wanted to take a great peace plan to all the Indians, a plan that would eventually bring all the tribes together into a parliament of nations. In Deganawida's vision he saw a gigantic spruce tree that reached its upper branches up through the sky to the endless light of the Elder Brothers. This tree, which grew out of a shining white carpet on the rocky hills, symbolized the sisterhood and brotherhood of all human beings. At its roots were the five nations of the original Iroquois confederacy. The soil that nurtured the roots of this tree was made up of three great double ideals:

1. Ne Skenno -- sanity of mind and health of body; peace between groups and individuals.
2. Ne Gaiihwiyo -- righteousness in deed, thought and conduct; justice and equity in the keeping of human rights.
3. Ne Gashedenza -- maintenance of military power for self defence; maintenance and increase of spiritual power.

Both Deganawida and Hiawatha, looking upon the human race as one great family, taught love and unity and obedience to God around many single family firesides. These single families formed the base from which the authority of leadership would rise. A marvelous structure was designed, making the individual families the center of power so that no dictatorship could seize power. The chiefs met to consult together with wisdom and maturity on all issues. Through prayer and humbleness they came to unanimous decisions.

Deganawida and Hiawatha saw that war was like the quarreling of children and they wished to end it. If the white men

had not come, they might have spread their plan of peace, understanding and love to many Indian nations, for there were
other Indians thinking along these same lines. In California
many tribes had learned to live in peace together, and in the
far-off southwest the Hopis (see page 53) were preaching the
brotherhood of man and peace to all Indians. Most of the Indian nations were made up of democratic social units, which
chose wise chiefs and leaders by merit alone, and avoided all
boasters and those who lusted after power. These social
units would have formed an excellent basis for a great democratic and peaceful confederacy of all Indian peoples.

So wonderful was the idea of Deganawida and Hiawatha
that the Iroquois confederacy of the five (and later six) nations
(the Tuscaroras joined later) was held together by it through
more than three centuries and it operates even today in spite
of all attempts of the white men to destroy it. The Iroquois
confederacy was, for long years, the most powerful group of
Indians in all of North America and many Indians besides the
Iroquois found shelter under its wings. Even the United States
government and its Constitution have many things borrowed
from the Iroquois, including the idea of the separation of powers of the judicial, executive and legislative branches of the
government. Thus flowered a great Indian genius.[43]

Unfortunately for the Indians the white men came and began to push the tribes against each other, supplying weapons
to some and urging them to attack others. Also the wars between the English, the French and the Spanish stirred up all
kinds of troubles, made worse by the bringing of whisky. But
Deganawida had another vision in which he foresaw this bad
time coming, although promising that eventually the spirit of
God would come to bring the Indians and all people to peace
and understanding. Mad Bear, a Tuscaroran, has given to
all of us this wonderful prophecy, as passed down from generation to generation in the long houses of the Iroquois:*

---

* *Originally printed in APOLOGIES TO THE IROQUOIS,
by Edmund Wilson; Farrar, Straus and Cudahy, 1959.*

"When Deganawida was leaving the Indians in the Bay of Quinte in Ontario, he told the Indian people that they would face a time of great suffering. They would distrust their leaders and the principles of peace of the League, and a great white serpent was to come upon the Iroquois, and that, for a time, it would intermingle with the Indian people and would be accepted by the Indians, who would treat the serpent as a friend. This serpent would in time become so powerful that it would attempt to destroy the Indians, and the serpent is described as choking the life's blood out of the Indian people. Deganawida told the Indians that they would seem to be lost, and he told them that when things looked their darkest a red serpent would come from the north and approach the white serpent, which would be terrified, and upon seeing the red serpent, he would release the Indian, who would fall to the ground like a helpless child, and the white serpent would turn all its attention to the red serpent. This bewilderment would cause the white serpent to accept the red serpent momentarily. The white serpent would be stunned and take part of the red serpent and accept him. Then there is a heated argument and a fight. And then the Indian revives and crawls toward the land of the hilly country where he would assemble his people together, and they would renew their faith and the principles of peace that Deganawida had established. There would at the same time exist among the Indians a great love and forgiveness for his brother, and, in this gathering, would come streams from all over -- not only the Iroquois, but from all over -- and they would gather in this hilly country, and they would renew their friendship. Deganawida said they would remain neutral in this fight between the white serpent and the red serpent.

"At the time they were watching the two serpents locked in this battle, a great message 'would come to them and make them ever so humble, and, when they became that humble, they will be waiting for a young leader, an Indian boy, possibly in his teens, who would be a choice seer. Nobody knows who he is or where he comes from, but he will be given great power, and would be heard by thousands, and he would give them the guidance and the hope to refrain from going back to

their land and he would be the accepted leader. Deganawida
said that they will gather in the land of the hilly country beneath the branches of an elm tree, and they should burn to-
bacco and call upon Deganawida by name when they are facing
their darkest hours, and he will return. Deganawida said that
as the choice seer speaks to the Indians, he would be heard by
all at the same time, and, as the Indians are gathered there to
watch the fight, they will notice from the south a black serpent
coming from the sea. He is described as dripping with salt
water, and, as he stands there, he rests for a spell to get his
breath, all the time watching to the north to the land where
the white serpent and the red serpent are fighting.

"Deganawida said that the battle between the white and the
red serpents would open real slow, but would then become so
violent that the mountains would crack and the rivers would
boil and the fish would turn up on their bellies. He said that
there would be no leaves on the trees in that area. There
would be no grass, and that strange bugs and beetles would
crawl from the ground and attack both serpents. He said that
a great heat would cause the stench of death to sicken both
serpents.   And then, as the boy seer is watching this fight,
the red serpent reaches around the back of the white serpent
and pulls from his a hair which is carried toward the south
by a great wind into the waiting hands of the black serpent.
As the black serpent studied this hair, the hair suddenly turns
into a woman, a white woman who tells him things that he
knows to be true, but he wants to hear them again. When
this white woman finished telling these things, he takes her
and gently places her on a rock with great love and respect,
and then he becomes infuriated at what he has heard, so he
makes a beeline for the north, and he enters the battle between the red and white serpents with such speed and anger
that he defeats the two serpents who have already become
battle-weary.

"When he finishes, he stands on the chest of the white serpent, and he boasts and puts his chest out like he's the con-
queror, and he looks for another serpent to conquer. He
looks to the land of the hilly country and then he sees the Indian standing there with his arms folded and looking ever so

noble so that he knows that this Indian is not the one that he
should fight. The next direction that he will face will be east-
ward, and at that time he will be momentarily blinded by a
light that is many times brighter than the sun. The light will
be coming from the east to the west over the water, and when
the black serpent regains his sight, he becomes terrified and
makes a beeline for the sea. He dips into the sea and swims
away in a southerly direction, and shall never again be seen
by the Indians.

"The white serpent revives, and he, too, sees this light,
and he makes a feeble attempt to gather himself and go toward
that light. A portion of the white serpent refuses to remain,
but instead makes its way toward the land of the hilly country,
and there he will join the Indian people with a great love like
that of a lost brother. The rest of the white serpent would go
to the sea and dip into the sea and would be lost out of sight
for a spell. Then suddenly the white serpent would appear
again on the top of the water and he would be slowly swimming
toward the light. Deganawida said that the white serpent
would never again be a troublesome spot for the Indian people.
The red serpent would revive and he would shiver with great
fear when he sees that light. He would crawl to the north and
and leave a bloody shaky trail northward, and he would never
be seen again by the Indians. Deganawida said that as this
light approaches he would be that light, and he would return
to his Indian people, and when he returns, the Indian people
would be a greater nation than they ever were before."

Comment on this prophecy.

Since this prophecy has been handed down through many
generations, some of the details may have been changed and
we cannot thus be sure of their meaning. However, there are
certain basic ideas that can be explained as follows:

1. The distress and sorrow of the Indians under the white
man's rule was foreseen by Deganawida, and has already
happened. This time of trouble took away the false pride of
the Indians and humbled them so that they are now prepared

to become spiritual leaders of mankind on the path to brotherhood.

2. All the Indians would begin to unite and work together
as they began to revive their old spirit. This spirit would begin to come back to them with the aid of a great new Message
from the east. This Message would be in perfect harmony
with all the good things in the old Indian religions and would
help bring the Indians together on the basis of understanding
and loving each other and these old religions.

3. The struggles between the materialist forces in the
world, as symbolized by the white, red and black serpents,
would not destroy the Indians because they would have found
both a material and spiritual sanctuary. The spiritual sanctuary itself would be so strong, due to the Indians becoming
great spiritual beings through their love and understanding,
that no one would dare attack them.

4. Deganawida said that he would return to the Indians
and that he would be the light coming from the east. We
must remember that the word "return" in this case can have
another meaning than the literal one. Just as Krishna, the
great Indian Prophet of India, said He would return (see page
37), and Jesus said He would return (see page 37), so Deganawida said he would return, but it should be understood that
a far more logical and intelligent explanation of this "returning" is that it means the return of the same spirit of God that
talked through these great Beings to men. We can thus see
that Deganawida foretold the coming of the great Prophet,
who would be the World Uniter who would bring true world
brotherhood. He would come with the same spirit of God that
was in Deganawida and Jesus and renew the spirit of man,
but in a way more worldwide and all-embracing than ever
before in history. It is not necessary for the Prophet Himself to come from the east to the west, but for His Message
to come. It is this Message, taught by dedicated teachers,
that transforms the hearts of men and creates a new earth.

F. VISIONS OF THE BLACKFEET AND OF AN ASSINIBOINE

Reproduction of George Catlin's painting of Indian camp.

1. Vision Witnessed by the Blackfeet people during their Sun Dance in one of the Last Years of the 19th Century.

The Sun Dance usually takes place in the middle of the summer months, and it can be best described as a time of supplication and thanksgiving to the Great Spirit. The Indians' holy men and women go into secluded lodges and fast from four to six days. During this time, they do not take anything to eat or drink, but spend their time offering prayers for the healing of all sicknesses, for the necessities of life, such as food, shelter and clothing, and for spiritual success and power. At the time of this particular Sun Dance, the Blackfeet were feeling very sad because almost all the buffalo, their chief food supply, had been killed, and they were being impoverished and oppressed by the white people.

The Sun Dance was well under way, with most of the Blackfeet people in attendance, when, during a time of prayer, the
skies were darkened by an approaching storm. As the people
looked in the direction of the sun, which was completely over-
shadowed by the turbulent black clouds, there was a sudden
and overwhelming stillness. Suddenly the clouds began to part
in every direction, and a round white cloud appeared in the
place of the sun. It, too, was moving, but it was coming
down towards them, towards the Sun Dance, and, as it came
closer and closer, it kept getting brighter and brighter. The
round form of the cloud kept changing and, as it got closer to
the encampment, it took on a form of a human being. When
it became visible to most of the people there, it stopped and
became suspended in mid-air. Then this cloud-like being
spoke in the tongue of the Indian people and told them, "- not
to be disturbed, but to be patient a little while longer, for He
would come again and lead them out of the darkness into the
light, and they would not suffer the same way again." In the
meantime, he told them to purify themselves by praying, and
by cleansing their bodies through the sweat baths, so that
when He returned they would be ready to receive Him and He
would live among them and guide them out of all their troubles.

(As told to Arthur and Lily Ann Irwin of Calgary, Alberta,
by a number of the Blackfeet people in 1962.)

2.   Assiniboine (Stony) Woman's Dream, 1962.

"(In my dream) I was walking through the woods looking for
some clean water to drink. I passed by many beautiful, green
meadows, but could not seem to find the water although I knew
it must be somewhere close by. I thought about my people
and knew that they were all right; they were not hungry any
more; they all had good warm homes with plenty of food and
sufficient clothing to wear. Still -- they all needed to find
the clean water for drinking.

"Wherever I went the little streams and lakes I saw were
muddy. So I kept on going, looking to the right and to the left.
I knew I must find it soon, maybe around the next meadow,

maybe after the next group of trees.   Every once in awhile I
would stop and think -- Maybe I am getting lost -- but no,
something inside me kept saying, 'Mary Jane, you must go
on!' All of a sudden I came to a good road with many green
trees on either side of it, and just around the turn of the road
there, on my left, was the most beautiful clear lake I have
ever seen.   I ran to the edge of the lake. I was so happy I
felt like crying because I had found the clean water at last.
As I knelt down to take a drink, I saw on the horizon of the
straight road ahead of me, a great big door opening into the
sky and all around the door the rays of the sun seemed to be
reaching far out into the deep blue.   Inside the door it was
very bright too, and the people of all races were there en-
joying themselves as if they were one big family.   With a
thankful heart I prayed to the Great Spirit my gratefulness
for His having guided me to this place.   Then I drank of the
pure water and walked up to the door on the horizon to join
all the people inside.   I felt so happy and peaceful because I
knew I had found what I was looking for.   As I stood at the
door, I thought about my people, and I knew I must first go and
tell my people to come and join us. "

(As told to Mrs. Lily Ann Irwin, of Calgary, Alberta, by Mrs.
Mary Jane Chiniquay, who, for forty years, had been a holy
Sun Dance woman of the Assiniboine.)

3. Comment on these two visions.

It is interesting that the Sun Dance Vision of the Blackfeet
came about the same time as the Vision of Wavoka, the Paiute
and Ghost Dance prophet (see page 62). Wavoka was told that
the spirit of Christ was on the earth. The Blackfeet were told
that the spirit of God would come to help them if they would
be patient. In all past history the Spirit of God has come to
mankind in the form of a great Prophet. This Prophet is usually rejected by men at first, because He does not come with
the physical glory they expect.   But slowly, and then more
and more rapidly, His great Message begins to spread over
the world and change the hearts of men.

We believe the Sun Dance Vision of the Blackfeet told them
that this new spirit had already come to the world, but that it
would be awhile before it would spread to them. It would be a
spirit of love and kindness and goodness among all races and
religions, for how else could the good days come back to the
Blackfeet if this were not so? They were only a small, minor-
ity people, oppressed by the white people. The hearts of the
white people would have to be changed. New teachers would
come who would give a Message that would be the same as the
presence of God Himself among the Blackfeet, since this Message would gradually change the hearts of men and produce a
new, spiritual civilization in which the rights and happiness
of all men would be fully protected. The Blackfeet, as well
as all Indians, should watch carefully for the coming of these
new teachers of love and unity.

The vision of Mary Jane Chiniquay was even more speci-
fic. She actually saw the union of all races in harmony, as
pictured in the sky. But how can this come about without understanding between the different races and religions? Only
a Great Prophet can bring this unity of understanding, for He
alone has the authority from God to explain the differences in
the religions and bring them together as One.

To Mrs. Chiniquay the pure water she was looking for obviously symbolized a new, pure religion, which her people
needed badly. This religion would actually fulfill the prophetic dreams of all peoples and all religions, breaking them
free from the walls that separated them and bringing them all
into loving harmony. Is this not what all the world needs?

G. HOPI PROPHETIC VISIONS

The very name Hopi means "the Peaceful People" and they have refused to fight against the white men. Even when they were thrown into prisons, as has happened many times, and even when treated badly in other ways', including having their lands stolen from them, the Hopi still have refused to fight back. But their spiritual power has been so great that they have maintained their village principles, their chieftanships and their religion despite the utmost pressure. Truly all Indians should be thankful that their Hopi brothers have been so successful in stopping the white men from destroying their culture and religion, because it is these Hopi who have best preserved the wonderful Indian spirit of the past.

Hopi girl in ceremonial costume, ready for dance. Field Columbian Museum.

The great Hopi prophecies have been handed down for many generations so it is possible, of course, that the wording has been changed here and there and the shades of meaning may have been altered a little. Like many prophetic dreams, these visions also have many symbolic meanings, so we have to be careful how we interpret them. We can, however, note and stress the main threads of the prophecies.

We give a shortened version here of these strange and beautiful prophecies.[48] Long ago, say the chiefs, Massau, the Great Spirit, told the Hopi to seek for a certain land to which

they would be led by a star.   In this land and on the tops of
the cliffs they would build their villages, up to four stories
high.   They were told that after a time strangers would come
(white men) who would attempt to take these lands and villages from them and who would often try to lead them into ways
that were bad.   This part of the prophecy has actually happened, as the white men have come and treated the Hopi and
other Indians badly.   But the Hopis were warned that, in spite
of all the pressures against them, they must hold to their ancient religion and hold to their land, though always without violence.   If they did this, they were promised that their people
and their land would be a center from which the Indians would
be reawakened.   Even now, by their example of kindness and
goodness and steadfastness in the Way of God, the Hopis are
showing all Indians how they must arise to change the hearts
of the white men.

The chiefs were told that the light that would bring this re-
awakening would come from the east and that it would come
from the True White Brother. He would wear a red cloak or
a red hat and would bring with him the sacred stone   tablets, which would be similar to the sacred stone tablet now
held by the Hopi, and which the True White Brother alone
could read.

The True White Brother, the Hopi believe, would bring
with him two great, intelligent and powerful helpers, one with
two signs like 卍 and ▽ and a hat shaped like ⌒ ,
while the other had the █ sign of the sun ☉ .   The com-
bined signs of the two helpers are painted on a sacred gourd
rattle of the Hopis, which is used in the Kachina Ceremonies
and looks like ⊛ .   The Hopis believe this gourd and its
signs represent ♈ the world and that when the great Purification Day is near, these helpers will shake the earth first
for a short time in preparation.   After they shake the earth
two times more, they will be joined by the True Brother, who
will become ONE with them and bring the Purification Day to
the world. All three will help the Younger Brother (the Hopis
and other pure-hearted Indians) to make a better world.   In
the prophecy, the two helpers are spoken of as if they were
large groups of people ("populations" is the Hopi word).

The Hopis were warned that if these three great beings failed, terrible things would happen to the world. Great numbers of people would be killed. However, it was said they would succeed if enough Hopis remained true to the ancient spirit of their people.

The THREE would show the people of the earth a great new Life Plan that will lead to Everlasting Life. The earth will become new and beautiful again, with lovely flowers, much animal life, and an abundance of food. Those who are saved will share everything equally. All races will intermarry and they will speak ONE TONGUE and be brothers. A NEW RE-LIGION will probably be brought that helps all people to lead better lives and transforms the world.

Comment on Hopi Prophecies.

There is much evident symbolism in the Hopi prophecies. It is wise not to take such symbols too literally, or the same mistake might be made as that made by the Jews two thousand years ago when they rejected their Messiah, Jesus, because He did not bring the literal power and glory they expected. The coming of a Great Prophet to any people, except those He is raised among, is the coming of His teachers. The Hopi and the other Indians need to look for teachers who bring the following ideas: one language for the world, a religion that fulfills the great principles of peace and understanding that is in the Hopi teachings and yet is also new, a religion that aims to end the destruction and exploitation of the earth by man, and end all war and violence, that seeks union and understanding between all races, and a religion that had its beginning in three great central figures.

The helpers of the Great Prophet can also be thought of as large groups of pure-hearted people who are spreading love, harmony and understanding between all races and all religions, humbly and without fanaticism. The New World of the spirit is coming, but there is much hard work ahead!

H. *THE GREAT DREAM OF BLACK ELK, HOLY MAN OF THE OGLALA SIOUX

"And I, to whom so great a vision was given in my youth -- you see me now a pitiful old man who has done nothing, for the nation's hoop is broken and scattered. There is no center any longer, and the sacred tree is dead." [45]

These are the words of Black Elk, the last of the great Sioux holy men, not long before he died. They are words that remind us of the Indians standing and lying, a broken people, on the hills in the "Strange Dream of the Oglala Sioux Pipe Bag" (see page 17). But remember how the white dove came and the Indians sprang up and marched into the sky, filled with glory and joy. If Black Elk could have fully understood his dream, he would not have been so sad.

That the Sioux also had forwarning of the coming of the white men in their dreams is told by Black Elk when he says that a very long time before the white men came there was a holy man called Drinks Water who dreamed that the animals were going back into the earth (meaning most would be killed) and that the Sioux would be ruled by a strange race who would make the Indians live in square gray houses in a barren land

* *Condensed version of dream told in BLACK ELK SPEAKS, by John G. Neihardt. University of Nebraska Press, used with the kind permission of the author and publishers.*

and that beside these square gray houses they would starve. This was exactly what happened to the Sioux during the bad years, particularly during the 1890's.

Black Elk was nine years old and camped near the Little Bighorn River in what is now Montana in the summer of 1872 when he appeared to become very sick and his strange vision came to him. He saw two spirit warriors with long spears tipped with lightning who came down from the sky like arrows and then carried him on a cloud behind them up into the sky.

Soon he saw the horses of the four directions, twelve black horses in the west, twelve white horses in the north, twelve sorrel horses in the east, and twelve buckskin horses in the south. Then he saw the whole sky filled with horses dancing and happy. He walked toward a white cloud and it changed into a tepee in which were seated six old men. These were the six grandfathers and the oldest called him to come inside and speak with them. He knew they were not truly old men, but the powers of the world, and he was filled with fear.

The grandfathers promised Black Elk several things. First they promised that he would make a nation, his nation, live, and second that he would have the power of healing. One grandfather showed him a bright red stick, from which bright green leaves sprouted, and told him that with this stick he would save many of his people. He was promised that he would have the power to destroy his people's foes. But he was also told that his people would walk the road of war and that they would have great troubles. However, in spite of these bad times, he was promised that he would help set the sacred stick in the center of the nation's hoop and make the people strong again. It was this part of the dream that later made Black Elk feel so sad, for he felt he had failed his people and that the nation's hoop was broken. But we believe that his vision and his help were vital to his people.

When Black Elk, in his dream, rode away from the six grandfathers on the bay horse the grandfathers gave him, he came along the black road that runs from east to west, the road of trouble and war. There he saw a blue man who was

turning the grass and the animals sick.   The horses of the
four directions attacked the blue man, but were driven back.
Then Black Elk rode to attack the man and speared him
through the heart.   There was a great cry of   "Un-hee!"
meaning he had killed, and suddenly the grass was green again
and the animals well and happy once more.

He believed he had been riding in the storm clouds and that
the earth below was suffering with drouth.   He came down from
the sky as rain and killed the drouth (the blue man).

After this Black Elk came to a village of his people where
all were sick and moaning.   But, as he rode through the village, the people rose well and happy behind him, all singing.
He gathered them together, and, following the command of a
voice, stuck the sacred red stick into the center of the nation's hoop, and the people shouted and sang with delight.
The wind blew gently, spreading deep peace.

Now Black Elk saw the daybreak star rising in the east,
and a voice said: "It shall be a relative to them, and who
shall see it, shall see much more, for from there comes
Wisdom; and those who do not see it shall be dark." The
people looked to the east, as the light of the star fell on them,
and all the animals of the camp called loudly.

These words, we believe, are among the most important
of Black Elk's dream, for they signify that a Message would
come to the Indian peoples from a great Prophet in the East,
bringing wisdom and good to those who would listen.   But all
who would not listen would remain in darkness.   The great
importance of these words is shown by the fact that after they
were said Black Elk saw the people take the road of goodness
and peace, the red road that runs from north to south.   They
were told that the grandfathers would now walk with them,
and the Great Voice said:

"Behold a good nation walking in a sacred manner in a
good land."

But Black Elk was warned that before this happened his
nation would walk through many difficulties on the black road

of trouble and war. He saw his nation scattering, each person following his own little vision while the winds of war sounded. This is the time in which the Indians are now, with the many little religious denominations, each narrowly saying it alone is right, and the many selfishnesses. After this Black Elk saw the nation's hoop broken and the people starving and in despair. But soon he saw a sacred man, painted red all over his body. This man planted a spear in the center of the people and then he turned himself into a fat buffalo (symbol of food and happiness and plenty). The spear turned into a beautiful sacred herb and the people began immediately to become better.

Black Elk understood then that the people would lose their contact with the Good spirit of the world and fall into a bad time, but they would get their strength and joy back again when once more they found that Good Spirit (symbolized by the bright red colored man and the sacred herb).

In another part of the dream Black Elk saw the people going through a great storm, a time of peril, but he was told he would be able to help his people through this time. He dreamed that he rode a sick and weak horse that turned into a great black stallion and a large number of horses danced around him. The big black stallion sang a beautiful song of a horse nation that shall be. Then Black Elk looked down from the sky and saw his people being blessed with friendly rain and a rainbow flaming in the east. This rainbow, we believe, symbolizes the Warriors of the Rainbow, the true brothers, who shall unite all the colors of the races into one harmonious whole.

Black Elk was carried to the top of a high mountain, and saw below him the hoop of the whole world and all the animals and people gathered together in love and harmony. He saw that the hoop of his own nation, the Sioux, was one of many hoops (of other nations) that made one great circle. In the center of the circle was a beautiful flowering tree put there to shelter all the people of the world, and he saw that it was holy.

At the very last of Black Elk's dream two spirit men came

to him and gave him the day-break star herb, the herb of understanding. He dropped it on the earth and it flowered beautifully, spreading its light over the whole world.

Finally Black Elk rose back through the sky to the   tipi of the Six Grandfathers and there he was told once more that he would help to make his people free.   Hundreds of his people, he was promised, would become as flames, spreading peace over the world. After this Black Elk dropped down from the sky and came awake in his parent's tipi.

Comment on Black Elk's Vision.

The central meaning of Black Elk's dream is very clear, for it is repeated over and over in different ways.   The people of the world shall go through a very bad time, a time of wars and troubles, a black road time.   Then they shall be awakened; their hearts will be enlightened and they will work to bring a good time to the whole earth, a time when all men learn to gather power and goodness from God. Here indeed is a wonderful vision of the future in which all the people will be gathered into the one fold and the one shepherd's flock, when all the many religions will become one big religion, with nothing narrow about it, big enough for all, and there will be no war any more.

Black Elk was told in his dream that the Message that would awaken and help his people would come from the east, and that it would come from a Man painted bright red (or clothed in red?). This man Black Elk met again later in another vision when he saw that He had long, flowing hair, but was like neither a white man nor an Indian in appearance. Black Elk saw that when the people received this new message, when they understood it, they would become like flames of fire, spreading it to other people.   But those who did not see the new Message would be filled with darkness.

The meaning here is very clear. The Indians should watch for this great Message of world unity with open minds, absolute faith and an abiding will.

61

I.

WOVOKA AND

THE GHOST

DANCE

The drawing
below is repro-
duced from an or-
iginal in the Bur-
eau of Ethnology,
Smithsonian In-
stitute, Washing-
ton, D. C.

Top, Wovoka,
by C. Sampson.

Bottom, Ghost
Dancers on plains.

Wovoka, the prophet of the Paiutes in Nevada, who brought the last Ghost Dance to the American Indians, was born about 1858 and lived until 1932. His great triumph came in 1890 and his great tragedy in 1891. In the previous January, 1889, he had had his famous vision, during which he lay as if dead for several days. When he woke up he felt glorified with the wonders he had seen. As Paul Bailey writes:*[41]

"For one solemn hour Wovoka, with tears streaming down his face, expounded the wonders of his vision. He had been to heaven. In a mystic land of great beauty, in which all the once-savage elements had been subdued and glorified, he had walked and talked with the spirits of the departed. There he saw the savagery of the wild beast reduced to the tranquility of lambs at play. He saw all Indians, of every diversity, and of every nation, walking arm-in-arm as brothers. He saw the flowering of physical beauty, the end of all pain and all disease, and man's final victory over death. And there the Indian was not the slave and the beaten dog of the white man, but stood in glorious dignity and equality with all. At the feet of these exalted beings, he had listened with reverence and with awe.

"'Go back to your people,' they had counseled, after Wovoka had pleaded to remain in this land of beauty and of peace. 'Go back, and tell your people the things that you shall hear. You must teach that Jesus is upon the earth. That he moves as in a cloud. That the dead are all alive again. That when their (the Indians') friends die, they must not cry. That they must not hurt anybody, or do harm to anyone. They must not fight. They must do right always. They must not refuse to work for the whites, and not to make trouble any more with them. You must take the dance we will show you back to the earth. It is the dance of goodness. It comes from heaven. It has a purpose. It will make your people free, and it will make them glad.' "

* Reprinted here from WOVOKA, THE INDIAN MESSIAH, by Paul Bailey; Westernlore Press, 1958, with kind permission of the publishers.

It has been popular to try to discredit Wovoka by pointing out that, according to some witnesses, he used magic tricks to fool the Indians into believing him, and that the dance he brought ended in despair when it did not bring the glorious future he predicted for the Indians. One popular view of the Ghost Dance, that Wovoka predicted it would drive away and destroy the white men, is, of course, utterly false. Other Indians, particularly the Sioux, Kicking Bear, and others of the Plains tribes, twisted the story to mean this, but they did this in their desperate desire to get rid of their enemies.

Essentially Wovoka taught the Indians that they must purify their hearts and do good deeds if they would change bad times into good times. The Ghost Dance was to teach harmony between all men, because even white men were invited to join in it and some did (see below). The mistake of most of the Indians, and possibly even of Wovoka too, was that they expected something good to happen immediately. They had been treated so badly by the white men that their need for a change for the better was desperate. But the pride and the hate many felt stood in their way like great walls. They had to learn to be humble and to love even their enemies. Wovoka tried to teach this, but the Indians were really not ready for this message. They wanted something more spectacular.

However, there are three reasons why we think the vision of Wovoka may have had something genuine in it:

1. First was his absolute sincerity with which he taught love and cooperation between the Indians and the white men plus his sincere urging on the Indians to give up their selfish ways and not blame the white men for their troubles. Selfish dreams do not fit this pattern (see page 85).

2. Second, Wovoka said the spirit of Jesus was in the world, but that he moved as in a cloud. The Bible speaks of the return of Jesus as a coming in clouds (Revelation 1:7) and like a thief in the night (Matthew 24:42-43). Is this not a warning that His coming would not be plainly visible, but in some way would be hidden? Why should we not use our intelligence to consider a different meaning for the idea of the return of Jesus besides the commonly and perhaps too blindly

accepted one that He is to visibly return with great material glory? If the same spirit of God speaks through a Man who is a great Prophet so that this is a spiritual return, not a per - sonal return, then it is perfectly possible for such a Man to appear among men who would not see His inner glory, since they would be foolishly looking for outward, physical glory. It is exactly in this way that Jesus originally came among men. Why not again? We believe it is perfectly possible that Wo- voka was telling the truth when he said Jesus (meaning, how- ever, the same spirit that was in Jesus) was in the world and was hidden by clouds. If this great Prophet were on earth at that time, He would probably be imprisoned and tortured by fanatical enemies, even as was Jesus. He would appear help- less to defend Himself, even as was Jesus. But He would send out a great Message of love and spiritual power that all men would eventually feel the force of and which would change hearts from evil to good until at last the world was changed to a new world of cooperation, justice and love.

3. It is very remarkable that in 1890 great numbers of white Mormons danced the Ghost Dance with the Indians.[41]   It was evident that they too expected a glorious event to happen soon. This was due to the strange prophecy of Joseph Smith (in his <u>Doctrine and Covenants</u>, 130:14-15), where he writes:[53]

"I was once praying very earnestly to know the time of the coming of the Son of Man, when I heard a voice repeat the following: 'Joseph, my son, if thou livest until thou art eighty- five years old, thou shalt see the face of the Son of Man; there- fore let this suffice, and trouble me no more on this matter.'"

If Joseph Smith had lived to be eighty-five years of age, this would have been the year 1890. If both Joseph Smith and Wovoka were right, the great Prophet was visible to men then. But the Mormons, like many other Christians, expected some- thing much more glorious, just as the Jews did in 30 A. D.

However, Joseph Smith had warned: "And when the times of the Gentiles is come in, <u>a light shall break   forth among them that sit in darkness, and it shall be the   fullness of my gospel. But they receive it not, for they perceive not the light, and they turn their hearts from me because of the precepts of men.</u> " (<u>Doctrine & Covenants</u>, 45:28-29).

So do men hear a message from God and refuse to listen!

IV. AN ESKIMO IN SEARCH OF GOD

By William Willoya

EARLY LIFE

I was born in Nome, Alaska, on July 11, 1939. My parents are mostly Eskimo, but with some white mixture. Our tribe was from King Island (Behring Straits) and Teller (on the mainland north of Nome). The white men thought of us as a primitive people with little learning, but we knew how to live in the ice and cold and snow of the far north where the white men died when they were cut off from their supplies. And before the white man came to us with his civilization we were a part of the spirit of God and the wilderness in a way the white man never understood.

Out of my childhood memories and dreams and meditations, also from the wisdom of the old people, the ones who knew the old ways, comes a spirit of love and tenderness that the Eskimo needs to give to the world. In this story, I want to form a bridge with my thoughts between the world of primitive man, the world of modern man, and the world that is to come.

The old, old lady who was my grandmother by adoption, filled the days of my childhood with a love that sang. She was a full-blooded Eskimo and had known the times before the white men came, the long-ago times when our hunters bravely hunted the walrus, the polar bear and the seal with spears

tipped with ivory or horn. As a four year old, she told me to
obey, for it would bring me its reward. As a six year old, I
can remember her kind, brown and wrinkled face smiling at
me with all the kindness and goodness in the world, and I remember her laughing most wonderfully when I brought her
my treasures from the sea, brown pieces of kelp, shells of
the big crabs, and stones whose bright colors caught my eyes.
When hurt or sick, she nursed me and soothed me so that the
touch of her hands wrote a music of tenderness. She died in
my eighth year, and that was a sad year, as if all the world
had ebbed away into the blackness of grief. But the memory
of her always remains, guiding me with her deep wisdom and
her knowledge of what the ancient people knew. For her love
fixed in me a bond with the life of the Eskimo that will abide
with me forever.

You who live in civilization, can you open your minds and
hearts and see with me the long Arctic nights, the long, long
darkness, when I and other little children sat in the flickering light of the seal oil lamps and looked up into the wrinkled
face of wisdom? Can you hear the cold Arctic wind howling
outside and banging on the walls, and hear also the strange
and wonderful stories of the old days coming from those lips
like streams of gold? We learned how the hunters rose on
the ice and threw their spears to draw the blood of the great
white bear, Nanook-soak. How the tribe nearly starved to
death when the seals withdrew somewhere into the blackness
of the great north, and skin was boiled to make soup, was a
frightening story. But, through all the stories, like a gold-
en thread, was the goodness of the people to each other,
their kindness and their thoughtfulness, their humble worship
of the Great Spirit, and their heroic sacrifices when danger
threatened.

She who was the heart and soul of my beginning told me
that my heart must always remain open and sincere, that I
was to live life to the fullest. She always told my mother and
me that meditation, sincere thinking about God, must be a
daily habit. Later I would know the meaning and value of this
when life would test me. When evil befell me, meditation and
prayer would be the cords that led me back to God.

Playing as a child and listening to stories and wisdom from the old one, my life was enveloped in a glorious world where troubles never seemed to come and people were always happy. But this changed when I went to the first grades in school and found myself shoved with other Eskimo and Indian children into separate buildings from the white children.

One day, when I was with a group of Eskimo children, some white children shouted names at us. I can still remember their faces twisting with meanness and the shrill hate in their shouts. Blinded with tears and the feeling I was not loved nor wanted, I asked my mother if I could leave this school with its separate racial buildings. All my favorite friends were leaving. Why could not I also go? Why do people have to be so ignorant and cruel? For a long time after that I looked on white people with suspicion; for a long time my childish life was filled with the nightmare of the white man's misunderstanding. The love of a protecting sister helped somewhat to ward off this outer world of unreason.

I turned also to nature, to the wilderness of the tundra and the rocks of the sea for help. The wild cry of the geese honking northward in the spring-time, the auks and puffins nesting in clouds on the rocks of the coast, the sight of the small furry lemmings darting through the short grass and the moss, all these reminded me that I also was a child of the Great Spirit.

But the scar of my first childish brush with the white man's intolerance and blindness would remain deep within me, making me in youth and early manhood cautious and withdrawn. For a long time I could not talk to a white man as one friend talks to another.

I talked to my school friends about this that troubled me, investigating their ideas. One of my friends told me that because the races were not really acquainted with one another yet, I should be patient. Another told me that life would always take on certain patterns; there would always be evil and misunderstanding. But I felt that somehow love one day would change things, that someday, when I could fill the shoes of the old ones, with their goodness and kindness, I could help bring this love to the world.

PROPHECIES AND DREAMS OF THE ESKIMOS

Eskimos always believed in God.   Our society existed around clans, around village principles of oneness and unity. Giving was a sign of love, meditation a sign of modesty, of the humbleness of man; thoughtfulness a sign of tact.   In the old days an Eskimo would go many miles to help a friend, would open his home wide to friend and stranger alike, but the Eskimos were astonished when the white men came and brought the good religion of Christianity and yet seemed to forget the tenderness, love and wide understanding of Jesus.

We knew life had mysteries.   God was good and we were to watch His plan.   He has given our people stone tablets for our guidance and protection.   We must not allow ourselves to stray from them, for God has always been good to us when we followed His loving teachings and loved Him and each other. But long before the white men came the old people were told in their dreams of strange invaders who would cover the land. During this bad time our people would be perplexed.   Some would stray from the good Eskimo teachings and practice bad things the strangers brought.

But my grandmother and other old wise ones told us that they had had visions of the coming glory of God and we would learn about it in good time.   We must sincerely search throughout the lands for a new Prophet.   We would know Him by His teachings, by the wonderful Message He brought, and the way He changed the hearts of men.   The old ones told us that 1912 had been a year of special significance in dreams. They were under the white man's heel then, but this would change.   They saw in their dreams a strange and wondrous white figure, a man with a flowing white beard and long flowing hair.   He would come from the east.   He wore a special kind of hat with cloth wrapped around and around.   This was not the great Prophet, but one who came from Him, who came to America as His messenger.

When I was twelve years of age I was praying and meditating.   I fell asleep and suddenly had a most wondrous dream. I saw in my dream the huge figure of a man, whose face was

filled with love, towering over all humanity with special ser-
vants beneath Him guiding the masses of the people to God.
This new religion, I was warned, would appear strange and
different at first, against many established ideas.

Not long after this some Eskimo friends told me that they
had dreams of me embracing Eskimo and Indian chiefs.   All
were happy, all were receiving a message from the Almighty
through me. I was an instrument used to tell them of the di-
vine whisperings for a New Age, brought by a new Prophet of
God. This deeply troubled and frightened me.   How could a
poor Eskimo youth, with so little power or gifts do this thing?
It was plain great humbleness was required.   My heart must
be purified of all pride and vanity and lust. To even think for
a moment of being better than others would destroy my value.

How amazing it was later to look into the very faces of the
Indians and Eskimos I had seen in dreams, for these same
dreams my friends had had came to me in the past few years
and guided me to those I sought.

A WARNING AND A PROMISE

As a youth I met missionaries and Christian preachers. I
was told about the Bible and its story and I read it. It was hard
for me to understand. What meaning could it have for an Eskimo? We always believed in God and practiced the law of
love, the brotherhood of man. Why did I have to study something so old? I believed my grandmother taught me just as
great wisdom, though she was not a Christian.   She told me
to expect a new prophet, but that I was to be content with what
the All-Knowing gave me. So I became a student of religion.

I found much that was good in Christianity, but, like other
Eskimos and Indians, I was astonished at the white men.
They had this beautiful teaching, but very few of them lived
by it. Even the preachers and missionaries often seemed cold
to me because they were so formal and self-righteous.   And
it was confusing that there were so many sects and denominations, each saying the others were wrong. Somehow Christianity was like a great puzzle that had broken into many little

parts. <u>Who was going to put the parts together again and make the puzzle whole?</u>

One day a minister told me that a new false prophet had a-risen. His followers preached the unity of all religions, say-ing that there was good from all of them that could be used by man, and that this would help them face the wrath of God. The preacher told me this was a bad religion because it bor-rowed other religious ideas, and because it did not exalt Jesus above all other prophets. I turned to the Bible to find answers to this question and found it told me that many false proph-ets would come, but that we would know them by their fruits. If the fruits were bad that they brought, then they would prove themselves to be false prophets. But if the fruits were good, then this would be a sign that they were from God. I prom-ised myself that I would test this prophet by his fruits when I learned more about him.

And, as I read the Bible, I saw also that many people of the time of Jesus believed He was a false prophet. They re-fused to believe in Him because He came in a different way than they expected and because he taught new ideas. They paid no attention to the fact that He led a life of goodness and of service to mankind. They also pointed to Scripture to "prove" He was false. So I saw that just because people told me a man was a false prophet was no proof that he was one, or even if they quoted sayings from the Bible to prove it.

I realized one who claimed to be a prophet had to be care-fully studied and tested with an open mind before one could judge him. The people of the time of Jesus had refused to study His teachings because they were so sure He was wrong even before they began to investigate Him. There is only one way to find the truth, I thought, and that is to work and study hard to find it.

MEETING THE FIRST OF THE NEW TEACHERS

A new start to my life came from my first meeting with a man whose whole life was so inspired, dedicated and devoted to the service of God, one of the new teachers of world unity and understanding. His message was brought to the north, to Nome, Alaska, in 1956.

He taught me an entire new concept, that in one's whole life one must live one's religion, including trying to love and understand all human beings one met without in the least degree looking down on them or condemning them. He also taught me to love and understand animal life, and that all men should seek for the truth without allowing other people to use pressure or fear or similar means to force them into any belief. So I began to ask this man about his church, if such it was, and what was their teaching on society and the world.   Was this just another of the cults coming into the north, such as the other Christian sects I had met.

I was told that the new Faith came from a new Prophet, that mankind was just beginning to feel the impact of his teachings, and that the opportunity to use my past as an Eskimo would now be tested. My first question was: "Does this Prophet believe in unity?" The reply was that He came to unite the kindreds of the world into one country and one religion through understanding and love. This appealed to me very much and led to more serious conversations, which reached a fever pitch.

Reflecting over my past I decided to study this new religion, and find if the Prophet was the one promised in all our legends. First, the test of time would prove if this religion was bearing any fruits, and secondly, the life reflected in the saintly character, purity of heart and individual conduct of this teacher would be another great measure of the truth that he brought.

I remembered how we Eskimo children were taught by the old ones that there would be a new Prophet of God, who would come from the east. He would come, we were told, when the world was asleep and badly in need of help. His Message would purify the souls, illumine the hearts and guide all people to love one another.

By questioning, I found that this was exactly the plan of the new Prophet. He taught that the walls of mistrust and misunderstanding between the religions were all made by men, who read into the teachings of their Prophets things that were not there, just as the Jews rejected Jesus because He did not bring what they wished. The new Prophet teaches all men to cast aside their petty thoughts and jealousies that keep them apart and grow big enough and whole enough to see that God has helped mankind in many ways and in different places all over the earth.

One of the great things I learned was that the new Prophet came to awaken the Indians and Eskimos and other dark skinned people from their bondage to and fear of western civilization. They must see that many people of this civilization are like little children who have wandered far from the path to God and are destroying themselves in a reckless search for riches and power. But deep in their hearts these people are unhappy and do not really know what they want. Before the world is destroyed by war and by exploitation and waste, the Indians must become filled with such a great spirit of understanding, love and kindness themselves that they will bring the power and riches-seeking people back from the brink of disaster and make them whole again.

So powerful is the spirit of God, now spreading over the world, said my teacher, that in this very generation we will see miracles of sacrifice, heroism and the changing of the hard hearts of men. This is a big thing, he said, so big that few can understand what is happening. The world will be literally exploded loose from the evils of narrow national, racial and religious jealousies by the work of increasing millions of human wills concentrating with all their might on bringing to the world understanding and love.

Meditating and thinking on all that I was told, I knew I must continue searching to make sure that He is the right One. I joined the army and toured Europe during 1958 and 1959. This experience caste the die that was later to make me sure that this new pattern of love, unity and understanding was what the world so desperately needed. I saw the

Christian churches hopelessly divided and separated by walls of narrow thought and doctrine that caused them to be pushed back and back by the waves of materialism and hate and prejudice that beset the world.   I desired from life more than the struggle of these broken fragments who needed the strength of wholeness and understanding. And I saw that never could they attain this until they recognized that God had sent a New Messenger, that the return of the Christ spirit had happened, but like a Thief in the Night, as the Bible foretold. How simple it was to understand when one saw that it was not the return of the same individual, but the return of the same spirit of God speaking through a Man.

ADVENTURES OF THE SPIRIT

My life attained a new horizon and a new insight when I came back to Alaska, for now my heart was afire with love and my mind with understanding. I attended Junior College in 1959-60, and this was the year that the love and gentleness of the new teachers finally convinced me that they brought the Message sent by God for this Age.   But they insisted that I must search entirely with my own mind and through my own careful investigation to find out if this was the truth.

One thing I had to learn and that is that people who joined the new Faith had to remake their lives in order to spread the new spirit across the world, and that some made this change more slowly than others, carrying into the new movement old habits and attitudes that were harmful.   Not until these people allow the full spirit of the new teachings to enter their souls do they become clean and beautiful within as God means them to be.

But the lesson of the way is there, just as it is and was in all the great religions, if we will only search for it and follow it.   The main difference between the new Faith and all previous religions is not in the teaching of the good life, I saw, for all taught people how to be good and kind and pure of heart. But the difference lies in the fact that new Way shows the path for all the religions, even the ancient religions of the Indian and Eskimo peoples, to understand how to love one another, and to put together the great puzzle that is religion into one complete and wonderful whole without fanaticism.

In my studying of the new religion, I traveled.   I went to Kotzibue and Kobuk and many other places that lie in the northern wilderness to learn more about my people, to see some of them as they were in the old days. I wanted to find out why the Eskimos were unique and what made them so happy, what made them so contented, when most of the rest of the world did not seem to have a moment of rest.   In their deep peace I found the new Prophet's Message reflected, for it also teaches the same inner peace, that makes a man stand still as a silent pool and say: "Here am I, Lord.   Do with me as you will." The Eskimos, the true Eskimos, live by giving joy to others and in this giving there is much contentment and much peace.

Now I prayed the wonderful new prayers as I traveled and they made my feet like wings.   To those who read them sincerely, they are filled with light and glory.   You can see in them the pure water of life eternal and the heavenly music of love. Let them flow into your heart and you will see that this music, these glorious words, come from God.   When I let them sing in my heart, in my mind, in my soul, without any pride, without any vanity, without selfishness, then I become afire with the New Message, and a humble servant of God.

WE INDIANS MUST ALL BECOME SEEKERS

Reflecting on the conditions of the world, the evil, violence, exploitation and despair, I suddenly thought: "Why cannot the Indian and Eskimo believe this new Message, since this is the same Prophet, the same principles, about which they were forewarned?" And I asked myself? "Why were they given warning?" Suddenly I knew! The Indians and the Eskimos were humbled by the white man's conquest of them. They were hurt and lacerated, torn and bloodied, by the bruising materialism of the white man's civilization. But out of their hurt, out of their grief, they can learn a deep lesson. God was actually preparing them for a great task that only they and the other dark-skinned races of the world with poor and primitive backgrounds can do. A job is given to the Eskimos and the Indians to bring unity and love to the world. It is in this way that God shall reward us for our suffering, and poverty, that we shall be spiritual giants, though humble before God and all men. This is our cup of mercy and we must share it with all who will accept it. All can learn to accept the almighty breezes of loving kindness that will create the brotherhood of man and a new earth.

MY TRIP THROUGH NORTH AMERICA
IN SEARCH OF OUR TRUE BROTHER

On July 26, 1961, I commenced a trip throughout Alaska, Canada and the United States to talk with the different Indian tribes and their chiefs. I came to tell them of the new Message, as well as to find out what they were doing about the surge toward unity of all Indian brothers. Especially I sought for those Indian brothers whose prophecies so closely were tied with those of the Eskimos that they too were now eagerly awaiting the New Message.

My dream of the true brothers was that they were desert Indians, very fast runners, and lived up on the cliffs like our (the Eskimos') forefathers. They would love the out-of-doors, would cultivate their fields, and would speak spiritual words similar to those used by my Eskimo people.

In Nevada I found Indians who spoke some similar words, but they did not fulfill the prophecy concerning the types of houses. They listened to my Eskimo talk and and said that the Hopi Indians of Arizona spoke a similar language, that they had stone tablets similar to the ones my village had kept for centuries, and expected the coming of the new age of mankind's progress toward light and knowledge.

Suddenly one of the friends said the Hopis would be having their Kiva Dances next winter, and then I asked what the word meant in English. The reply was: "Kiva means social hall or meeting place." This was all I needed to convince me that probably I had now found where my true brothers live, since the word "Kiva" means the same thing to my Eskimo people.

We left early in September and soon arrived in Hopiland to visit the chief, a man of great dignity and kindness, who welcomed us with deep friendliness. As I looked into his wise eyes I knew I had at last found the one who would release the bonds of my heart, fulfilling the end of the last revelation of the Eskimo prophecy. As the prophecy said, we would not only understand each other, but we would see how our paths merged and became one. This was the great path to world unity to be followed by all the Indian peoples.

What a joy filled my heart on that day!!! Talking only a few minutes with the chief, my happiness soared to the clouds, for this great spiritual leader's boundless wisdom and knowledge convince me that at last I had found our true brothers in Hopiland. Their customs were similar, the clan order, also the sanctity of the chieftainship was honored in the same way, and all the requirements for the final fulfilling of our great spiritual instructions were obeyed.

I wanted to dance, so great was the joy that overflowed into the mesas! We went over many of the instructions for the final consumation of the unity that would be asked of all Indians during this time of the end of one age and the beginning of another. We had to accomplish the unity of the Indians in order to usher in the new era of unity for all mankind. We saw the clouds of glory advancing and all the Indian peoples marching with us to the titanic victory of justice and freedom and peace for all the peoples of the world!

V. THE TASK OF THE
WARRIORS OF THE RAINBOW

We have seen the golden thread of the prophecies that foretell the day of the awakening of the Indian peoples and the formation of a New World of justice and peace, of freedom and God. We have seen how the Warriors of the Rainbow (the new teachers) are prophesied to come and spread this great Message all over the earth. But how are the Indians going to help these prophecies come true?

For long years the Indian peoples have been sleeping, physically conquered by the white people. For all this time they have been taught to believe that the white men were superior to them, that they must learn to live in and become a part of this white civilization, as it exists, even if a lowly part. It will not be easy to awaken them from their sleep. It can be done if we realize that the Indians are sleeping giants, that within each of them are marvelous powers of the spirit that need only be started into action to create miracles of work done for the good of all and deeds of shining heroism.

The world is sick today because it has turned away from The Great Spirit.[55] [56] When men turn once more to the Ancient Being with love and world understanding, the earth will become beautiful again. [61] Indians can help mankind to return to the Wise One Above by obeying the following principles.

Like the great Indians of old, they will teach unity, love and understanding among all people. They will listen no more

to the little people who say they alone have the truth, but shall
see that He Who Listens to All is too big for little things, too
full of justice to accept but one self-chosen people, too free
to be caged by any mind. They will listen instead to those who
teach harmony between all men, even as the wind blows without favoritism into all the corners of the world.

Like the pure Indians of old, they will pray to the Spirit
with a love that flows through every world even as the breeze
sings its song to the Silent One among the needles of the pines.[5]
In solitude and in council their hearts will lift with joy, free of
the quarrels and petty jealousies brought by men, free to love
all mankind as brothers. As the Great Spirit loves a smile and
happiness, they shall sing of the coming glorious union of men.

Like the glorious Indians of the past, by their joy, by their
laughter, their love and their understanding, they shall change
all men whom they meet. Like the rushing torrent of a river that wears away the hardest rocks, they shall wear away
the hardest hearts with love, until the whole world begins to
bloom with the new growth of man.

Like the radiant Indians of old who strengthened their muscles by hard exercise and then nourished their souls by fasting and prayer, so shall they make themselves heroes of the
new age, conquering every difficulty with the strength of their
bodies, the fire of their love and the purity of their hearts.
Filling their mouths with only pure foods and liquids, and
seeking the beauty of the Master of Life in every thought, they
shall scorn harmful drinking and unclean habits that destroy and
weaken men. They shall run to the hilltops to pray and fast and
into the solitudes of the forest and desert to find strength.

Like the Indians of old who let their children run free in
the prairies, the woods and the mountains to help them grow
into men and women worthy of their Creator, so the Warriors
of the Rainbow today shall work to bring to all children the
magic blessing of the wild, the delight of bare feet running
through green grass over the hills, and the cool touch of the
wind in their hair. The spiritual civilization that is coming
will create beauty by its very breath, turning the waters of

"THE PEYOTE DREAMERS," Al Momaday (Kiowa). The fire, s
bird in glorious color is the return of the spirit; the feathers s
its signal of the concentration of the mind upon spiritual

SPIRITS OF THE NIGHT," Tzo Yazzie (Navajo). In the brooding
n the spirit over a child of the New Day, and the girl cradles
e the oneness of the Indian with all living things.

THE OGLALA SIOUX PIPE BAG,
photo by Charles Bello. This bag
symbolizes the purity of the spirit
in man.

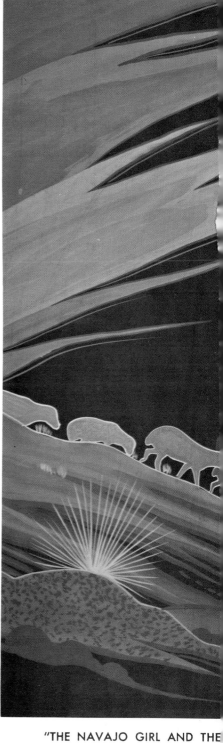

"THE NAVAJO GIRL AND THE
darkness the Old Ones hover
a lamb to symboli

AL MOMADAY

rrounded by its curved moon of dirt symbolizes purity; the peyote
ymbolize the touch of the Great Mystery; the drum will beat out
hings; the peyote button (center) brings the gifts of the spirit.

rivers clear, building forests and parks where there are now deserts and slums, and bringing back the flowers to the hillsides. What a glorious fight to change the world to beauty!

Like the Indians of old who loved, understood and knew the powers of animals and plants, who killed or took no more than they needed for food or clothing,[5] so the Indians of today will brighten the understanding of the ignorant destroyers. They will soften the hearts of would-be killers so the animals will once more replenish the earth, and the trees shall once more rise to hold the precious soil. In that day all peoples shall be able to walk in wildernesses flowing with life, and the children will see about them the young fawns, the antelope and the wildlife as of old. Conservation of all that is beautiful and good is a cry woven into the very heart of the new age.

Like the kind Indians of old who gave work to all and kept care of the poor, the sick and the weak, so the Warriors of the Rainbow shall work to build a new world in which everyone who can work shall work and work with joy and with praise of the Great Spirit. None shall starve or be hurt due to the coldness and forgetfulness of men. No child shall be without love and protection and no old person without help and good companionship in his declining years.

Like the joyful Indians of old, the new Indians shall bring back to their own people and spread to other races the joy of good-fellowship and kindness and courtesy that made the life in the old Indian villages such a happy time for all.[15]   How they danced together! How they ate together in loving harmony! How they prayed together and sang together in joy![15] It shall come again and better in the new world.

Wise Indians do not speak without reason and they shame a boaster by their silence; so today the Indians shall teach all people to make their deeds count bigger than their words. Deeds of love and kindness and understanding shall change the world.

Even as the wise chiefs are chosen, not by political parties, not by loud talks and boasting, not by calling other men names, but by demonstrating always their quiet love and

wisdom in council and their courage in making decisions and
working for the good of all.[43] So shall the Warriors of the
Rainbow teach that in the governments of the future men will
be chosen out of the ranks by quality alone and then will counsel together in freedom of thought and conscience. In counsel
they shall seek truth and harmony with hearts full of wisdom
and prefer their brothers to themselves.

Among the Indians of old, children and youth respected the
elders and were taught love and unity, strength of character,
love of the Great Chief in the Sky and good deeds from babyhood.
Today young people, who should be the hope of mankind, have
wandered far from this strength of soul in their pursuit of pleasure and "success." The Warriors of the Rainbow will bring
back this lost spirit before it is too late and the youth shall
once more do great deeds of selflessness and heroisim. The
glory and the purity of their lives shall light the world.

The thoughtful and devoted chiefs of old understood their
people with love; the parents of old educated their children with
love; all new Indians will associate with other religions and
peoples with love. One minute of such love and understanding
brings wealth from the Great Spirit and creates miracles of
accomplishment. It is love then with understanding that the
Warriors of the Rainbow will mix in their medicine to heal the
world of its ills, leavened with pure hearts and humble minds.

Those who do not understand think that when their Messiah comes He will do their work for them. But always, when
a great Prophet comes to the world to change the hearts of
men, he calls for heroes and those who work with happiness
and dedication. Great are the tasks ahead, terrifying are the
mountains of ignorance and hate and prejudice, but the Warriors of the Rainbow shall rise as on the wings of the eagle
to surmount all difficulties. They will be happy to find that
there are now millions of people all over the earth ready and
eager to rise and join them in conquering all barriers that
bar the way to a new and glorious world! We have had enough
now of talk. Let there be deeds.

"The morning stars sang together, and all the sons of God
shouted for joy." Job, 38:7.

APPENDIX

A. WILLIAM WILLOYA

By Vinson Brown

When I met William Willoya, the Eskimo, I was sure I had met a man. Willy stands six feet one inch tall, with the broad shoulders and muscles of a true athlete. He has been toughened by hard work on Bering Sea fishing boats, as a hunter of seal on the ice and of caribou over the barren tundra of the far north. However, it was plain to me that Willy was a bigger man than I ever was, not because of his size and strength, but because of what I saw in his eyes.

Willy has very black and very quiet eyes, questioning when he first meets you, testing you. Those eyes are very direct. They seem to look right through you and understand you. But those eyes are wonderful when Willy smiles. Willy smiles with his whole face. His face comes alive and almost seems like the sun. Then his eyes are warm and filled with lights, little dancing lights of friendship and kindness. You can see way down inside Willy and see the good, warm, strong heart that is there. When you see that you understand that Willy is a Big Man, a really BIG MAN.

I knew that Willy would be of much greater value in the writing of this book than I would be, because the Eskimos are very close to the Indians in feeling and outlook. Willy has been to the Hopi Reservation in Arizona and found that the Hopi people have a spiritual language similar to his language and have sacred stones remarkably similar to the sacred stones the Alaska Eskimos have.

A second reason why Willy is vital to our story is because he has met and talked to many hundreds of Indians in his travels over Alaska, western Canada and the United States. Because he is one of them, he has learned their troubles, their dreams and their visions. How wonderfully now he can help them.

Another reason why Willy can be of such help is because he still has a lot of the old Indian Spirit, the spirit that comes from living in the wilderness, from living close to nature. There is a great power in this spirit, a power about which the white men know little. Willy's people live way up near the top of the world, near the North Pole. Half of the year they live in darkness or near darkness because the earth has turned so that the sun's light no longer reaches the far north lands. The Eskimo have to hunt through the darkness and the ice and the snow for seal and walrus, polar bear and caribou. Often they may not be able to find food for days or even weeks, so these people seek sustenance from the Spirit of God to help them stay alive. Because they know always that God is near to help those who seek Him with love, they are a happy and joyful people even though they live in the midst of danger and disaster.

Even the white men, with their materialism and their lack of sensitivity to the beautiful thoughts and ideals of the Indians and Eskimos, have not been able to kill this wonderful spirit of the Eskimos. This bigness of the spirit, as Willy points out, cannot find any lasting shelter within narrow denominationalism or a dogmatic religion that refuses to see other points of view.

B. THE PEYOTE RELIGION

The Peyote Religion, which also is called The Native American Church, is an example of the need of the Indian to understand religion in his own way.[6] [8] [13] Members of this religious movement believe in Jesus and the Bible as coming from God, but also believe that God sent to the Indians the Peyote Woman, who brought to them the peyote drug, used in their ceremonies. The drug, when taken properly, with prayer, meditation and singing, brings visions to the Indians who use it, and they say gives them directions and warnings from God. The peyote button is taken from a cactus plant found in Mexico and the southwestern United States. It is chewed, but has a bitter taste. The peyote ceremony is generally held in a tipi, with a circle of Indians inside, led by the Peyote Chief. A half moon of ashes, a drum and various other ceremonial helpers (some of which are shown in our color plate) are used. The ceremony usually lasts all night, with considerable singing and drum beating.

The visions of those who take peyote are often very strange and beautiful, as shown in our color plate. Colors of most brilliant shades may appear and usually pulsate, probably in tune with the beat of the Peyote Drummer. The fantastic experience gives evidence of transforming and improving character when tied in with religion, but there seems to us to be some danger that Indians and others who use peyote might come to depend on the drug too much, and not enough on their own efforts. The purification of the hearts of men requires hard work and anything that helps this is good, but should not be depended upon alone. Certainly peyote should be used with great care, particularly as there is evidence it may be harmful to some people, and not used at all where it is against the law.

There is considerable controversy over whether the drug compounds found in peyote are harmful or not, though most authorities are agreed that they are not habit-forming.[11] Use of the drug even in religious ceremonies is banned in some states, but in Arizona recently the State Supreme Court declared the law an unconstitutional infringement of religious freedom. Followers of Peyote teach the leading of a life of purity. In fostering ceremonies that use some of the old Indian ideas of religion, they probably help preserve and rebuild some of the wonderful old Indian spirit that the Indians were losing. Some of the Peyote dreams have been of a time coming when all peoples would be united in brotherhood. If true, then Peyote itself is a step in this direction, and the followers of this religious movement are being made ready for something bigger and wider that will bring all peoples together in love and harmony.

C. THE PROPHECY OF PROUDHON

A great and sensitive Frenchman, Pierre Joseph Proudhon, wrote a prophecy in the 1860's about the white man's civilization. He said:*

"Today civilization is in the grip of a crisis for which one can find only a single analogy in history - that is the crisis which brought the coming of Christianity. All the traditions are worn out, all the creeds are abolished;

* *Quoted by Erich Fromm in his book, THE SANE SOCiety (Rinehart).*

but the new program is not yet ready, by which I mean that it has not yet entered the consciousness of the masses. Hence what I call the dissolution is here. This is the cruelest moment in the life of societies. -- I am under no illusions and do not expect to wake up one morning to see the resurrection of freedom in our country, as if by a stroke of magic. No, no; decay, and decay for a period whose end I cannot fix and which will last for not less than one or two generations -- is our lot. -- I shall witness the evil only. I shall die in the midst of darkness.

"Europe is sick of thought and order; it is entering into an era of brute force and contempt of principles. Then the great war of the six powers will begin. Carnage will come and the enfeeblement that will follow the blood baths will be terrible. We shall not live to see the work of the new age, we shall fight in darkness; we must prepare ourselves to endure this life without too much sadness, by doing our duty."

The great wars have come that Proudhon foretold and the many troubles. But now, at last, more and more people of all races are awakening to the vital need for love and understanding between all peoples and religions. And a great new religion, free of all the centuries of accumulation of built-in prejudices and narrow doctrines and dogmas of the past, has now come to mankind, fulfilling the prophecy of Proudhon of the coming of the new program, and giving us the tools with which to build a new and glorious world.

D. SCIENCE AND PROPHETIC DREAMS

Scientists have long been very reluctant to allow the possiblity of there being any truth in prophetic visions or anything else that happens outside of the five senses. A simplified statement of Sigmund Freud, the great Austrian psychologist, is probably a good example of this feeling:

"There can be no doubt that prophetic dreams can be said to exist in the sense that they deal with man's thoughts directed into the future. It is doubtful, however, whether these thoughts or visions show, in any exact way, the actual future events. I confess that, in this case, my policy of having an open mind has deserted me. I do not believe any mental effort other than shrewd calculations by a man of wide-spread knowledge would be able to see future events in detail. That dreams by people who do not have such knowledge should do so is both opposed to scientific expectations and attitudes, on the one hand, and corresponds far too closely with ancient and well-known human wishes, on the other hand, for scientists not to reject such an idea as all but impossible. It is my belief, therefore, that if we add to the often reported unreliability of such dreams, the fact that often their meanings are changed after events have happened, and that even sometimes they are correct by accident or coincidence, we will find that their value from the standpoint of science amounts to almost nothing. I personally have never experienced anything that could cause me to change my mind about this view." [3]

The answer to Freud and other scientists who take this viewpoint is that the whole history of science shows how often supposedly reputable scientists have made such judgments as this because of lack of sufficient evidence and have later been proved to be very wrong. Admittedly the study of prophetic dreams is still in its infancy, and its water is muddied by many false dreams and much nonsense, but this is no excuse not to investigate with an open mind.

Our purpose in this book, as is that of any interested scientist, is to try to find out if there is any way, in a logical and reasonable manner, to find patterns and laws or rules that may help us understand prophetic dreams. We frankly admit that our investigations of this matter form only a beginning, and that future facts that come to light may cause us to change our conclusions. But a start must be made.

Scientifically we should look for patterns in visions that are repeated at widely separate places and times, because such patterns can show us laws of prophetic vision behavior that may go far to prove the existence or non-existence of a force and purpose behind them. But we should realize that parts of visions often appear in symbolic terms and we need to search for keys that will help us unlock the meanings of these symbols. Thus the rainbow that ends one part of Black Elk's vision (see page 59) probably symbolizes several things: (1) peace after the storms of war and suffering, (2) God's covenant with mankind through His Prophets, and (3) the union of all the colors of the races of mankind in pleasing harmony. We also need to watch very carefully for adulterations or other changes in prophetic dreams made by later writers or story tellers. Here a vast amount of research is certainly needed and we have but scratched the surface. A suggestion on how fakes can possibly be detected is explained in the next section.

In studying prophetic dreams, which are a form of extra-sensory perception, we are dealing with the subjective mind of man, something that is very hard to pin down under ordinary scientific terms or investigations. When a man prays wholeheartedly to God and receives great help and power through his prayers, what scientist can define exactly what this power is or put it into any kind of graph or diagram? Yet, surely, the history of mankind again and again shows evidence of the the existence of this power. Dozens of great spiritual leaders and doers have accomplished miracles through this power and transformed the hearts of millions of men. Modern science has tried to ignore these facts because it did not understand them, but the time for such ignorance and avoidance is now over.

In this book we use our deep inner feelings to give you our subjective appraisals of the strange prophecies and visions we are writing about. This subjective analysis may not qualify as science, but it can be stated as a scientific hypothesis which future discoveries and future events may or may not prove to be wrong or be right. We do know that prophetic visions in the Bible, such as the prediction of the dispersal of the Jews and their final return to the Holy Land (Nehemiah 1:8, Jeremiah 23:3), have actually come true in a remarkable way. Only time will tell whether the prophecies you find in this book will come true or not, but we hope you will keep your mind open and will never stop seeking for the truth. Remember that the great bulk of new ideas brought to the world, and particularly those in the religious field, have been rejected by men without honest investigation due to the emotional conditioning of the human mind by old dogmas, superstitions and ideas, which have become out of tune with reality. Modern man cannot afford to make this mistake in the perilous age in which we live.

E. UNDERSTANDING THE SYMBOLOGY OF PROPHETIC DREAMS

Many of the great historical events of mankind have been connected · with prophetic dreams.[54]   If we can study these events carefully, we may be able to understand those patterns of thought that show how prophetic dreams prepare the way for history. Not only this, but we may be able to see also how prophetic dreams have been misinterpreted in the past and so avoid   this misinterpretation in the present.

Since a large percentage of prophetic dreams have had to do with   the coming of a great world religious leader, or messiah, it would seem wise at first to try to show the difference between a true messiah and a false messiah.   There is, of course, one school of thought, exemplified by   the athiests, the non-believers in God, who say there never has been a true messiah. We cannot get into an argument with the athiests at present,   because this is outside the scope of this book, but we can say that we believe one of the great proofs of the existence of God is that there is a peculiar type of great Man, illustrated by such prophets as Moses, Buddha and Jesus, who have had a spiritual impact on hundreds of millions of people over centuries of time and have influenced their lives so as to create great civilizations,   in which cooperation between men has been responsible for their success, and lack of cooperation has spelled their downfall.   A STUDY OF HISTORY, by Arnold Toynbee, the famous historian, illustrates this in detail in   twelve, magnificent volumes.[61] We can therefore define a true messiah as follows:

The true messiah changes the lives of millions of human beings over centuries of time by teaching them the love and understanding that causes them to cooperate with each other, thus producing the flowering of civilization. Religious prejudices alone prevent men from admitting that the following great Men have done exactly this: Krishna (the founder of Hinduism), Zoroaster (the founder of Zoroastrianism and the wonderful ancient Persian civilization), Moses, Buddha, Jesus and Muhammad.

The false messiah, on the other hand, can be defined as a man who makes the claim that he is the messiah, come to liberate a particular people or the world, but fails in one way or another to produce any good effect upon history, or at least no lasting effect of any consequence.   There have been literally hundreds of these false messiahs.[49] [52] [54]

Having defined the nature of the true and false messiahs, it is necessary to define the nature of messianic expectations, so we can understand why and how both true and false messiahs have been received by the people who are expecting them. Messianic expectations have had their original source usually in the definite statements of great prophets that they would return, or in the prophetic visions of seers or lesser prophets. These dreams and statements are either reproduced in books, such as the Bible, or handed down from generation to generation as traditions, such as the tradition of the return of Quetzalcoatl told by the Mexican Indians.

One factor evident in many of these prophetic dreams and statements is the idea that the original great Prophet will return again.   Thus Krishna said He would return and so did Jesus. It is a factor of messianic expectations that millions of people have expected a literal return of the exact same individual even though, historically speaking, this has never happened.   The return, so far as any logical explanation of it is concerned based on actual,

historical happenings, has always been a return of the spirit, speaking again
with the same power, but through a different Prophet.

Another factor of the messianic expectations is that people have expected
the Messiah to produce miraculous signs to prove that He is a true messiah.
Again, historically speaking, these signs have rarely appeared, and so the
messiahs have usually been rejected, even though later the influence of their
love and teachings on the world have changed the hearts of millions and created new and brilliant civilizations.

With the possible exception of Muhammad, who did answer the   dreams
and expectations of the Arabs in a way that satisfied them, most messiahs
never have fulfilled the messianic expectations of the people of their time,
because they have not come in the literal way and with the literal power and
glory expected.   The people have not understood that the signs they expected were largely to be taken symbolically and that the Great Spirit did not want
them to judge a prophet or messiah by outward power and glory, but by the
beauty of His inward spirit and His deeds of kindness, goodness and wisdom.

Scientifically we can show that all such blindness towards the coming of
the Spirit of God is due to emotional conditioning. Every human being is subject to more or less emotional conditioning when he is young. Millions of
people, for example, are emotionally conditioned to fear all snakes because,
when they were young, some adult, usually the mother, showed great emotional fear toward a snake found by the child.   Since the great majority of
snakes are completely harmless, this emotion has very little to do with reality.   In the same way most people are emotionally conditioned when they are
young to look with suspicion on any other religion except their own and may
even be told stories to reinforce this prejudice, stories that far too often are
based on misunderstanding. Thus are the blind of spirit created.

The Jewish Prophetic Dream of the Messiah

One of the great prophetic dreams of all history was the Messianic dream
of the Jewish people that is told about in the Old Testament of the Bible.[49][52]
This dream is mentioned again and again in such passages as Daniel, 9:25
(when even the date of His coming is given), Isaiah 9:6, and so on.   There is
a curious double nature, however, about these prophecies, because close study
shows that they are speaking of at least two different comings of a messiah.
The last one is the World Uniter, the Prince of Peace, foretold also in the
prophecies of other religions.

Since Jesus Christ came at the time prophecied in Daniel, and since His
healing Message of love has gone out and spread to hundreds of millions of
people all over the world, creating a great world civilization, the Christians
believe that this is proof that Jesus was the Messiah for that time. The Jews,
however, are still waiting for the coming of their Messiah, for they say that
a Prince was supposed to come to them with great power to free them from
their bondage.   They forgot that their Bible also prophecied that they would
be cast out of the Holy Land and be driven all over the world because of their
rejection of the Voice of God (see Ezekiel 36:19, Leviticus 26:33, Deuterono-
my 4:27, Nehemiah 1:8, Ezekiel 12:15, and so on).

It is interesting to note that though the Jews rejected Jesus and refused to
follow Him because He did not fulfill their prophecies in the literal way they

wanted (that is, He did not come with great physical power and glory), they did several times rise in great numbers and follow false prophets or "messiahs" who misled them with promises of physical power and glory. Judas, the Zealot, in 68 A. D., Bar Kochba in 117 A. D., and Sabbathai Zvi in 1666A.D. were only a few examples of numerous such "messiahs." All were eventually defeated severely by foreign armies and their dreams proved unanswered, or were discredited in other ways.[54] [1]

Note that these people desperately needed a messiah, but that again and again they accepted the leader who brought them what they thought would be physical glory, completely neglecting and ignoring the true Messiah, Jesus, who would have brought them something much more important, spiritual glory. Nevertheless, there is one good excuse the Jews have had for rejecting Jesus, and that is that there is evidence that the Christians themselves sometimes twisted the teachings and descriptions of Jesus in such a way as to make it almost impossible for the Jews to accept Him.[5] This was due largely to the influence of the mystery religions of the Roman Empire, which made a culture hero or prophet synonymous with a god and had developed the idea of the physical resurrection of the god-man or prophet. Thus many of the Christians made an equal of God out of Jesus, despite His own denial that He had any power aside from the Father (see <u>Matthew</u> 19:17 and <u>John</u> 8:28).

Other Examples of Prophetic Dreams from History

Another people who dreamed of a messiah who would save them from their conquerors were the Welsh of the land of Wales in what is now called the British Islands.[54] The Welsh had a prophetic dream told to them by Merlin, a famous seer or visionary who lived about 525 A. D., that they would be conquered by a foreign people (the English), but would someday have back their ancient glory. A few centuries later the English conquered the Welsh, and held them under their rule until the present day. But several times in history Welshmen arose who said they had dreamed they came to fulfill the Merlin prophecy. Each time the Welsh rose to throw out the English, and each time the Welsh were severely defeated and reconquered, thus proving their mistaken interpretation of these dreams. Note that the interpretations of the dreams were selfish, seeking material glory for the people and leader.

The Indians have had many men arise and say they had prophetic dreams of how the Indians would drive the white men out of America. The Shawnee, Tenskwatawa (called "The Prophet") had such a dream about 1800 and tried to rouse the Indians to revolt against the whites, but his dream failed. Two other Indians who taught such prophetic dreams were Smohala, a Wonapan Indian dreamer of the Northwest, and Kicking Bear of the Sioux. Both said the dead Indians would soon rise to help the live Indians drive out the white men, but, in both cases, nothing happened to fulfill these prophecies. We can see that these interpretations of dreams were selfish, for they involved war and hate between the races.

In the Old Testament, in the Book of Genesis (<u>Genesis</u> 17:20, 21:13 and 21:18), there is a triple prophecy that the children of Ishmael, the first born son of the Prophet Abraham, would be blessed and that one day God would make them into a great nation. Since the children of Ishmael became the Arabs, as both Jews and Christians agree, this prophecy was not literally and completely fulfilled until the Prophet Muhammad came in the seventh century A.D. and united all the Arabs into a great nation for the first time in history, producing the wonderful Moslem civilization of the 8th to 11th centuries. It is true that later the Moslems did cruel things to the Christians and this started the great wars called the Crusades, in which the Christians struck back by doing cruel things to the Moslems, and much hate was roused between the two religions. But Muhammad had told His people to be very kind to the Christians and Jews, and Jesus, of course, had told the Christians to love their enemies and to be kind to those who despised them. So both Christians and Moslems forgot the teachings of their own prophets.

It is very remarkable that this very clear prophecy of the coming of Muhammad as a Prophet of God (for God blessed Ishmael and said He, God, would make Ishmael's descendants into a great nation) is in the Holy Books of both the Christians and the Jews. And yet both Jews and Christians refuse to recognize this triple prophecy because of their emotional prejudice against the Moslems. This kind of emotion obviously prevents people from thinking clearly and is one of the big reasons for misunderstandings between men.

Many of the true prophetic dreams of history have been forewarnings of trouble coming. Thus many Indian peoples had warnings of the coming of the white men as their conquerors. Drinks Water, ancient holy man of the Sioux (see page 56), warned of this. So also were the Mayas warned,[20] the Incas,[21] and other Indian nations. In reading the Bible, we can see that it is full of many prophetic visions by Jeremiah, Isaiah and other Jewish prophets of the coming scattering of the Jewish people all over the world because of the pride and blindness of the Jews. All of these dreams actually came true.

But notice also that many such prophetic dreams also prophecy a good time coming after all the trouble, a time when all peoples will be joined in love and harmony (see Isaiah 43:5 and 66:18, for example). Since the first part of these dreams (as also that of Djojobojo, given on page 33) came true in their exact details, it is reasonable to suppose that the second part will come true also, particularly when we have the same pattern of true prophecies of trouble repeated all over the world in widely separate places that could, in earlier times, have had no contact with each other.

We can now establish tentative rules that should help us understand some of the meaning of prophetic dreams so we can know something of the differences between them and of their symbolism.

RULE NUMBER ONE: We should be wary of dreams which advocate hate between nations, races or religions since history shows that these dreams have almost universally caused more harm than good.

RULE NUMBER TWO: There are hidden meanings in prophetic dreams and these are often more important than the literal meanings.

RULE NUMBER THREE: Emotional prejudices cause people to reject a prophetic dream even when it comes true. Therefore, we must get rid of all such emotional prejudices, which we have probably learned in childhood from adults who tried to blind our eyes to anything with which they did not agree. If we do not learn to understand these immature emotions and control them, it will be much more difficult for us to find the truth.

RULE NUMBER FOUR: A prophetic dream that foretells a time of great trouble for mankind that does come true, but foretells also a time of harmony among men that is to come later fits into a world-wide pattern. We should watch and study such dreams with great care, for this story is not repeated so widely among so many different peoples without reason.

RULE NUMBER FIVE: Since messiahs who fulfilled prophetic dreams in the past have generally fulfilled these dreams by bringing a spiritual or inner glory to mankind, rather than an immediate outward material glory, we can state that the major symbology of prophetic dreams is the putting of spiritual meanings into physical or material terms or symbols. We should, therefore, look for the spiritual, inward beauty of a Great Prophet, including the wisdom with which He tackles the problems of the world, instead of for outward glory.

F. HOW PROPHETIC DREAMS FIT INTO PATTERNS

The chart below shows how the great prophetic visions told about in this book, along with some other famous prophetic dreams, fit into certain definite patterns that are repeated over and over. Scientists search for laws of nature by studying such patterns, and we may similarly find laws of religious development or comparison behind the patterns shown here.

O. T. = Old Testament. N. T. = New Testament + = prophecy given	O.T. prophecies	N.T. prophecies	Blackfoot	Black Elk	Buddhist	Djojobojo	Deganawida	Eskimo	Hindu	Hopi	Montezuma	Mormon	Plenty Coups	Quetzalcoatl	Zoroastrian	Muslim
Bad time coming	+	+	+	+	+	+	+	+	+	+	+	+	+			
Spirit of people scattered	+	+	+	+	+	+	+	+		+	+	+	+			
Great wars	+	+		+	+	+	+			⊥						
Many little religions	+			+	+	+						+				
Messiah coming	+	+	+	+	+	+	+	+	+	+	+	+		+	+	+
Messengers come from east	+	+	+				+	+		+		+		+		
Messengers come from west						+	+			+						
Red clothing		+		+	+											
Unites religions	+	+		+	+	+				+	+	+			+	+
Freedom & God	+										+	+	+			
Unites races	+	+		+	+	+	+			+		+				+
People spiritually blind	+	+		+	+		+	+		+	+	+	+			

NOTE: the patterns of the messengers coming shows that the light of the new religion comes from east of the Holy Land and west of India. The map on the next page shows this more clearly.

Notice how often the same pattern is repeated over and over in many widely separated parts of the world. When we see all these patterns together on one chart it is like seeing a vast puzzle being put together in which a significant drama of human history is being laid out before our eyes.

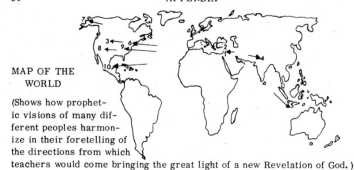

MAP OF THE
  WORLD

(Shows how prophet-
ic visions of many dif-
ferent peoples harmon-
ize in their foretelling of
the directions from which
teachers would come bringing the great light of a new Revelation of God.)

   1.   Old Testament prophecy of Ezekiel (43:2) foretells that "the Glory of
God came from the way of the east, and the earth shone with his glory. "
   2.   A New Testament prophecy in Matthew 24:27 foretells that: "For as the
lightning comes from the east and shines as far as the west, so will be the
coming of the Son of Man. " The great Prophet or His Message or both would
come to the Holy Land from the east this prophecy plainly foretells.
   3.   Black Elk saw a light coming from the east and was told that   wisdom
would come from that direction. (See page 58.)
   4.   The Buddhist prophecies of the Himilaya Mountains north of India foretold that the new teachers of a great prophet would come from the west. (See
page 41.)
   5.   The vision of Djojobojo, Javanese King, promised the coming of light
from a great spiritual King in the west. (See page 34.)
   6.   Deganawida of the Iroquois prophesied the coming of a great light from
the east that would change the World. (See page 47.)
   7.   The Eskimos of Alaska were told that a new prophet would send His
Message to them from the east. (See page 71.)
   8.   The Hopi prophecies foretell the coming of a message from the east.
(See page 55.)
   9.   In his Doctrine and Covenants 43:22 Joseph Smith, the Mormon prophet, explains that the new Message from God will come as "when the light-
nings shall streak forth from the east unto the west, - . "
   10.   Quetzalcoatl, the prophet-king of the Toltecs, said the return of the
spirit that spoke through him would be from the east. [12]

Quetzalcoatl, prophet-king of the Toltecs,
scarifying legs in penance for sins.
Old Aztec print.

On Dreams, Visions and Prophecies

1. Festinger, Leon, Henry W. Ricken and Stanley Schacter. When Prophecy Fails; University of Minnesota Press, 1956.
2. Freud, Sigmund. Collected Works, Vol. III, Dreams, page 180. Pantheon.
3. Lewinsohn, Richard. Science, Prophecy and Prediction. Harper and Brothers, 1961. Pages 99, 114, 123 and 139 are specially significant.
4. Lincoln, J. Steward. The Dream in Primitive Culture. Crescent Press, Ltd., London. Page 252, Mandans foresaw coming of guns and horses.

On Indian Religions

5. Alexander, Hartler Burr. The World's Rim, Great Mysteries of the North American Indians. Univ. of Nebraska Press, 1953.
6. Barnett, H. G. Indian Shakers, A Messianic Cult of the Pacific Northwest. Southern Illinois Univ. Press, 1957.
7. Black Elk. The Sacred Pipe, Black Elk's Account of the Seven Rites of the Oglala Sioux. Edited by Joseph Brown. Univ. of Oklahoma Press, 1953.
8. Deardorff, Merle H. The Religion of Handsome Lake; Its Origin and Development. Smithsonian Inst., Bur. of Am. Ethnology, Bulletin 149.
9. Recinos, Adrian. Popul Vuh, The Sacred Book of the Ancient Quiche Maya, English Version. Univ. of Oklahoma Press, 1950. See page 230.
10. Sejourne, Laurette. Burning Water, Thought and Religion of Ancient Mexico. Vanguard Press, 1960. Page 3 and 40 significant.
11. Slotkin, J. S. The Peyote Religion. The Free Press, 1956.
12. Spence, Lewis. The Religion of Ancient Mexico. Watts & Co., London, 1945. Pages 94 and 98, prophecies of Quetzalcoatl.
13. Steward, Omer C. Washoe-Northern Paiute Peyotism, A Study in Acculteration. Univ. of Calif. Publ. in Amer. Anthropology, Vol. 40, No. 3, 1944.
14. Wolf, Eric. Sons of the Shaking Earth. Univ. of Chicago Press, 1959.

On Indian Tribes

15. Alford, Thomas Wildcat. Civilization, as told to Florence Drake. Univ. of Oklahoma Press, 1936. See pages 52 and 56.
16. Debo, Angie. The Road to Disappearance. Univ. of Oklahoma Press, 1941. A story of the Choctaw Nation.
17. DeOnis, Harriet (translated by). The Incas of Pedro de Cieza de Leon (author). Edited by Victor Von Hagen. Univ. of Oklahoma Press, 1959.
18. Ewers, John C. The Blackfeet, Raiders of the Northwestern Plains. Univ. of Oklahoma Press, 1958.
19. Flornoy, Bertrand. The World of the Inca. Vanguard Press,1956. P. 25.
20. Forman, Grant. The Five Civilized Tribes. Univ. of Okla. Press, 1958.
21. Grinnell, George Bird. Blackfoot Lodge Tales, the Story of a Prairie People. Charles Scribner's Sons, 1903.
22. Hagen, Wm. T. The Sac and Fox Indians. Univ. of Oklahoma Press, 1958.
23. Haines, Francis. The Nez Perces, Tribesmen of the Columbia Plateau.
24. Hyde George Red Cloud's Folk. Univ. of Oklahoma Press, 1937. A History of the Oglala Sioux.
25. Hyde, George E. A Sioux Chronicle. Univ. of Oklahoma Press, 1956.
26. Hyde, George E. Indians of the High Plains. U. of Oklahoma Pr., 1959.
27. Hyde, George E. Spotted Tails' Folk, A History of the Brule Sioux. Univ. of Oklahoma Press, 1961.

28. Kennedy, Michael Stephen (edited and with introduction by). The Assiniboines, From the Accounts of the Old Ones, Told to First Boy (James Larpenteur Long). Univ. of Oklahoma Press, 1961.
29. McReynolds, Edwin C. The Seminoles. Univ. of Oklahoma Press, 1957.
30. Matthews, John Joseph. The Osages, People of the Middle Waters. Univeristy of Oklahoma Press, 1961.
31. Murray, Keith. The Modocs and their War. Univ. of Oklahoma Press, '59.
32. O'Kane, Walter C. The Hopis, Portrait of a Desert People. Univ. of Oklahoma Press, 1953.
33. O'Kane, Walter C. Sun in the Sky (a story of the Hopi). Univ. of Oklahoma Press, 1950.
34. Portilla, Miguel Leon (edited and with an introduction by). The Broken Spears, the Aztec Account of the Conquest of Mexico. Beacon, 1962.
35. Sonnichsen, C. L. The Mescalero Apaches. U. of Oklahoma Press, 1958.
36. Thompson, J. Eric. The Rise and Fall of Maya Civilization. Univ. of Oklahoma Press, 1954.
37. Vaillant, George C. Aztecs of Mexico. Doubleday, 1941.
38. Wallace, Earnest and E. Adamson Hoebel. The Comanches, Lords of the South Plains. Univ. of Oklahoma Press, 1952.
39. Wallace, Lew. The Fair God (An Account of the Conquest of Mexico by Cortes, seen through the eyes of the Indians). 1871. (Note: we have not been able to find the original source of the prophecy of Montezuma, given in this book, but even if it is a poetic vision of 1871, it still has value, as Wallace had a deep and loving insight into the character of the Aztecs.)

On Individual Indians

40. Bailey, Paul. Walkara, Hawk of the Mountains. Westernlore Press, 1954.
41. Bailey, Paul. Wovoka, the Indian Messiah. Westernlore Press, 1957.
42. Cornyn, John H. (translated from the Aztec by). The Song of Quetzalcoatl. The Antioch Press, 1931. Pages 44-48 give prophecies.
43. Henry, Thomas. Wilderness Messiah (the story of the Iroquois prophet, Deganawida). Wm. Sloane Assoc., 1955. Pages 25, 32-33, 37, 39.
44. Linderman, Frank B. American, The Life Story of a Great Indian (Plenty Coups, Chief of the Crow). John Day Co., 1930.
45. Neihardt, John G. Black Elk Speaks. Univ. of Nebraska Press, 1956.
46. Sandoz, Mari. Crazy Horse, The Strange Man of the Oglalas. Alfred A. Knopf, 1942.
47. Vestal, Stanley. Sitting Bull, Champion of the Sioux. Houghton Mifflin Co., 1932.

On Messiahs

48. Independent Hopi Nation. The Hopi Message, 2nd Edition. Published September 13, 1961, in mimeographed form.
49. Klauxner, Joseph. The Messianic Idea in Israel. Macmillan Co., 1955.
50. Mataram, Dihimpon O. T. Peranan Ramalan Djojobojo Dalam Revolusi Kita. Published by Masa Baru, Bandung, Indonesia, 1958.
51. Miller, David Humphreys. The Ghost Dance. Duell, Sloan & Pierce, 1959.
52. Silver, Abba Hillel. A History of Messianic Speculation in Israel. The Macmillan Co., 1927.
53. Smith, Joseph. Doctrine and Covenants. Published by Church of Jesus Christ of Latter-Day Saints, 1928. Prepares for coming of Messiah.

54. Wallis, Wilson D. Messiahs, Their Role in Civilization.   American
Council of Public Affairs, 1943.

Miscellaneous Books

55. Berrill, N. J. Man's Emerging Mind. Fawcett Publications, 1955.
56. Brown, Estelle Aubrey. Stubborn Fool, A Narrative. The Caxton Prin-
ters, 1952. A worker among Indians describes the killing of the spirit.
57. Fromm, Erich. The Sane Society. Rinehart, 1955.
58. Hanna Willard A. Bung Karno's Indonesia, Revised Edition. American
59. Sachar, Abram Leon. A History of the Jews. Alfred A. Knopf, 1948.
60. Sorokin, P. A.   The Crisis of Our Age. E. P. Dutton and Co., 1941.
Shows the great disaster brought to our age by too much materialism.
61. Toynbee, Arnold J. A Study of History, in 12 volumes. Oxford University Press; Vols. 1-3, 1934, Vols. 4-6, 1939, Vols. 7-10, 1954,   Vol.
11, Atlas and Gazetteer (by Toynbee and Myers), Reconsiderations, 1961.
Abridgements of first 10 volumes in 2 volumes, by D. C. Somerwell.   A
penetrating, sympathetic view into world history (much related to religion).

On World Religions

62. Burtt, E. A. (edited by). The Teachings of the Compassionate Buddha. A
Mentor Book, 1955. Beautiful thoughts in beautiful prose.
63. Charavarty, Amiya (edited by). A Tagore Reader. The Macmillan Co.,
New York, 1961. Hindu religion reflected by a great Indian poet.
64. Conze, E., I. B. Horner and A. Walley (edited by).   Buddhist Texts
through the Ages. Philosophical Library, 1954.
65. Ferraby, John. All Things Made New, A Comprehensive Outline of the
Baha'i Faith. George Allen & Unwin, Ltd., 1957.
66. Kraemer, Hendrik. World Cultures and World Religions.   The West-
minster Press, 1960. A Christian approach to World Religions.
67. Pickthall, Mohammed M.   The Meaning of the Glorious Koran, An Ex-
planatory Translation. Mentor Books, 1953. Explains Moslem Religion.
68. Prabhavananda, Swami and Christopher Isherwood (translated by). The
Song of God, Bhagavad Gita. Mentor Books, 1944. Hindu Religion.
69. Rhys Davids. The Digha-Nkaya in Sacred Books of the East.
70. Sears, William. Thief in the Night. George Ronald, 1961. A comprehensive search for the missing millenium.

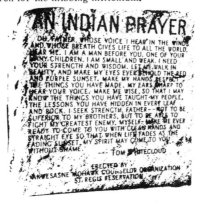

94   ACKNOWLEDGMENTS

We would like to acknowledge some kind and proficient help in preparing this book from the following people: Mr. David Peri of Santa Rosa, California, an anthropologist who is part Miwok Indian, and who was good enough to carefully read and criticize the entire manuscript; Mr. Henry Crow Dog of Rosebud, South Dakota, who checked on elements of the story of the Sioux pipe bag; Mrs. Lily Ann Irwin of Calgary, Alberta, who helped us with the Blackfoot and Assiniboine stories; Mr. Harry Roberts of Guerneville, who gave to us a breath of the spirit of the Yurok people in north-western California, of whom he had been a member; Mrs. Marie Potts, a wonderful Maidu Indian lady of Sacramento, who gave us her reaction to the story; the family of Mr. and Mrs. Dionisio Reos, Pomo Indians, who kindly listened and made suggestions about the book; Mr. Thomas Banyaca of Hotevilla in the Hopi Reservation in Arizona, who looked over the Hopi chapter; Mr. Ray Fadden, Secretary of the Akwesasne Mohawk Counselor Organization of Hogansburg,   New York, who sent us the beautiful prayer of Tom White Cloud, Objibway; and all our wonderful Indian artists whose work in this book breathes the old Indian spirit in all its glory.

INDEX

CANADIAN BAHA'I
DISTRIBUTION SERVICE
7290 LESLIE ST.
WILLOWDALE, ONT.